THE SPIRIT of
C.S. LEWIS

Also edited by Lesley Walmsley and available from HarperCollins*Publishers*

C.S. Lewis on Faith
C.S. Lewis on Grief
C.S. Lewis on Joy
C.S. Lewis on Love

THE SPIRIT *of*
C.S. LEWIS

A Year of Readings from
His Life and Work

Edited by Lesley Walmsley

 Fount
An Imprint of HarperCollins*Publishers*

Fount is an imprint of HarperCollins*Religious*
part of HarperCollins*Publishers*
77–85 Fulham Palace Road, London W6 8JB

First published in Great Britain in 1999 by Fount

A catalogue record for this book is
available from the British Library

ISBN 000 628078 1

Printed and bound in Great Britain by
Woolnough Bookbinding Ltd, Irthlingborough

Contents

Introduction

TO FIND THE 'SPIRIT' OF SOMEONE whom you have never met is a chancy business, for what speaks to me may not speak to everyone else, and others may regret things which I have left out, sometimes simply for lack of space.

The extracts in this book are, with one exception, taken from Lewis's own writings, the exception being Warren Lewis's simple account of the day his brother died. They are also generally placed within the months in which they were originally written or published, and each month can be taken as a separate entity. However, life is not tidy enough to proceed through the span of twelve months in a completely chronological way, so this book does not present the story of Lewis's life from birth to death in that order. Others already do that well.

An outline of the facts is that Clive Staples Lewis was born into the family of a Belfast solicitor in November 1898, the younger of two sons. His life was spent as an academic – mostly in the University of Oxford, where he lectured in English – and he is famous now for his writings on Christianity.

That is an outline of his life, but what makes his spirit? There is the little boy with his own study, deciding to become a writer because his hands were too clumsy to make things. He had earlier shown another part of his individuality by announcing that he wished to be called 'Jacksie', and thereafter was always known as Jack. There is the glimpse of what he came to call 'Joy' when his brother Warnie brought him a garden on a tin tray, and his whole delight in 'Northernness'.

After the emotional devastation caused by his mother's early death came the trauma of life at boarding schools in England, but these difficult experiences were followed by the dawning delight of real academic study, under the tutelage of W.T. Kirkpatrick. He was an extraordinary man from whom Lewis learned how to question everything and to order his daily life in such a way as to make the most of every hour.

Beneath all this was the troubled love that Jack had for Albert, his eccentric, lonely and sometimes gloomy father, and his unquestioning love for his brother Warnie. Three years his senior, Warnie was the rock of the young Jack's life, and was to remain his best friend until Jack's death in 1963.

Mr Kirkpatrick foresaw that Jack was destined to lead an academic life, and in 1917 he went up to Oxford, though his stay there was short-lived because he was soon called up to serve in the army in France. After the War Jack returned to Oxford and entered into university life enthusiastically, and with distinction. He published his first book of poems when still only 20.

When Jack joined the army he met Paddy Moore, and on Paddy's death in action Jack fulfilled his promise to look after Paddy's mother and sister – a promise that he kept for many long years. Life in their strange household put a great strain upon Jack, and his father was greatly annoyed by the situation.

After the day's work, Jack's evenings were spent discussing all kinds of subjects with some of the finest minds of his generation, and such debate with a group of friends was to remain one of his greatest pleasures. The group was known as 'The Inklings', and over the years its members included other writers such as J.R.R. Tolkien, Charles Williams and Owen Barfield. Puzzled by the fact that so many of these brilliant thinkers were Christians, after many months of debate, in 1931 at the age of 32, Jack himself was finally converted to belief in Jesus Christ as the Son of God.

The fact that he had worked through all the arguments against Christianity for so long, the very lucidity of his mind, and his command of clear English made Lewis an ideal person to speak about Christianity on the radio. His first series of radio talks, called *Right and Wrong*, was broadcast by the BBC in 1941. The talks were warmly received, and other radio series followed in subsequent years, all finally to be published together as *Mere Christianity*, the most popular of Lewis's adult religious books.

His academic work and his writing went on, and then in a civil ceremony in April 1956 Jack married Joy Davidman, an American divorcée with two sons. At first no more than a typically kind gesture by Lewis to allow her to remain in England, their friendship grew, under the shadow of Joy's illness, into love and then into a true marriage after a religious ceremony when Joy was ill in hospital. The man hitherto seen as a confirmed bachelor blossomed as a husband and stepfather, receiving perhaps the final blessing on an already full life. They had a relatively short time together, but a happy one, and after Joy's death Jack wrote *A Grief Observed*, one of the most open books ever written on the subject.

The Britain in which Lewis lived was very different from the Britain of today in many ways, but especially with regard to travel and communication. Although some people did have cars, walking was still very popular, and longer journeys were made by trains and buses. Lewis, of course, crossed by boat when he went home to visit his father in Belfast, and it was not until July 1957, going for a holiday in Ireland with Joy, that he first flew. Communication was by letter (or by telegram in cases of real emergency), and it is fortunate that so much of the Lewis correspondence still remains. Telephone calls were made sparingly, and there were, of course, no computers or fax machines to send electronic messages around the world. Television was not widely available until the late 1950s, so radio played an important part in people's lives, especially during the Second World War. Radio talks were broadcast live, from London rather than Oxford, which meant that Jack had to travel back and forth by train each time, instead of dropping into a local studio, as would be the case today.

He lived in a world that was different to ours, but the things that Lewis wrote about still speak clearly to us today. By the time I started reading his books it was already too late to meet him, but they have given me a picture of a strong man; a brilliant mind; a generous friend; an academic who nevertheless worried about domestic arrangements at home; a person who took the time to answer carefully letters from all kinds of people (he had the rare gift of writing well to children); a Christian who daily lived out his beliefs; a man who loved to walk and talk and laugh with friends; a gifted speaker and writer who loved the English language and could use it splendidly; a fully rounded man of the sort one comes across but once in a lifetime; and a Christian author whose writings have never been surpassed.

Reading his diaries and letters, and trying to follow his thoughts, I almost feel that I did meet C.S. Lewis. I hope that this book will introduce him to you and lead you to get to know his spirit for yourself.

Lesley Walmsley

January

IN BRITAIN JANUARY IS A MONTH when the daylight hours are short, when outdoors there may be snow, ice and gales, but indoors the comforting warmth of home or study is at its best. There is something about a new year, a fresh start, which fills most of us with expectancy, with a sense that *this* year we shall do things better, achieve more, be better people. January was a month in which a lot of things started for C.S. Lewis, either symbolically or in fact, beginning with his baptism as an infant in 1899. And it was in January 1942 that he gave his second series of radio talks for the BBC – *What Christians Believe* – which later were to form part of his best-selling adult religious book *Mere Christianity*, which itself was to prove a start in faith for so many people.

On a more personal level, it was in January 1950 that he received the first letter from Joy Davidman, who was to change his life so much; and it was in January 1951 that the burden of caring for the ailing Mrs Moore was lifted when she died.

In January 1946 *The Great Divorce* was published, while January 1964 (a few months after Lewis's death) saw the publication of *Letters to Malcolm: Chiefly on Prayer*, a manuscript which his publisher greeted as 'The best you've done since *The Problem of Pain*.'

One of the great elements in Jack Lewis's life was his search for what he called 'Joy', and without an understanding of what he meant, one cannot find his spirit. Here he gives some of his early experiences of 'Joy' and tries to describe just what it was. Later in life he was finally overtaken by Joy and was, albeit reluctantly, converted to belief in a loving God.

At the age of six, seven and eight I was living almost entirely in my imagination … Certain … experiences were [imaginative] … The first was itself the memory of a memory. As I stood beside a flowering currant bush on a summer day there suddenly arose in me without warning, and as if from a depth not of years but of centuries, the memory of that earlier morning at the Old House when my brother had brought his toy garden into the nursery. It is difficult to find words strong enough for the sensation which came over me; Milton's 'enormous bliss' of Eden (giving the full, ancient meaning to 'enormous') comes somewhere near it. It was a sensation, of course, of desire; but desire for what? … and before I knew what I desired, the desire itself was gone, the whole glimpse withdrawn, the world turned commonplace again, or only stirred by a longing for the longing that had just ceased. It had taken only a moment of time; and in a certain sense everything else that had ever happened to me was insignificant in comparison.

The second glimpse came through Squirrel Nutkin; *through it only, though I loved all the Beatrix Potter books … It administered the shock, it was a trouble. It troubled me with what I can only describe as the Idea of Autumn … And one went back to the book, not to gratify the desire … but to re-awake it. And in this experience also there was the same surprise and the same sense of incalculable importance …*

The third glimpse came through poetry. I had become fond of Longfellow's Saga of King Olaf: *fond of it in a casual, shallow way for its story and its vigorous rhythms. But then, and quite different from such pleasures, and like a voice from far more distant regions, there came a moment when I idly turned the pages of the book and found the unrhymed translation of* Tegner's Drapa *and read*

I heard a voice that cried,
Balder the beautiful
Is dead, is dead …

I knew nothing about Balder; but instantly I was uplifted into huge regions of northern sky, I desired with almost sickening intensity something never to be described (except that it is cold, spacious, severe, pale, and remote) and then, as in the other examples, found myself at the very same moment already falling out of that desire and wishing I were back in it …

The quality common to the three experiences … is that of an unsatisfied desire which is itself more desirable than any other satisfaction. I call it Joy, which is here a technical term and must be sharply distinguished both from happiness and from pleasure. Joy (in my sense) has indeed one characteristic, and one only, in common with them: the fact that anyone who has experienced it will want it again. Apart from that, and considered only in its quality, it might almost equally well be called a particular kind of unhappiness or grief. But then it is a kind we want. I doubt whether anyone who has tasted it would ever, if both were in his power, exchange it for all the pleasures in the world. But then Joy is never in our power and pleasure often is.

Surprised by Joy

In January 1919, after the end of the First World War, Lewis returned to Oxford to resume his studies. Still only 20, he already had behind him the experience of being wounded during the fighting in France, but knew that he was lucky to return to England alive, when many of his companions were dead. Life in Oxford had changed since his first taste of it, and a fortnight later he wrote to tell his father how things now were.

After a quite comfortable journey (which showed me that first class travel is very different from third) I arrived here somewhat late in the evening. The moon was just rising: the porter knew me at once and ushered me into the same old rooms … It was a great return and something to be very thankful for…

There is of course already a great difference between this Oxford and the ghost I knew before: true, we are only twenty-eight in College, but we DO dine in Hall again, the Junior Common Room is no longer swathed in dust sheets, and the old round of lectures, debates, games, and whatnot is getting under way. The reawakening is a little pathetic: at our first [meeting of the JCR] we read the minutes of the last – 1914. I don't know any little thing that has made me realize the absolute suspension and waste of these years more thoroughly …

The coal difficulty is not very serious. We have all our meals in Hall, which, if it abolishes the cosy breakfast in one's rooms and the interchange of 'decencies and proprieties' is a little cheaper: we shall go back to the old arrangement as soon as we can. The library, one lecture room, and the Junior Common Room are always warm, and the two former are quite quiet: then for the evening we can afford a modest blaze at one's 'ain fireside'. Our little body gets on very well together and most of us work. The place is looking more beautiful than ever in the wintry frost: one gets splendid cold colouring at the expense of tingling fingers and red noses.

Letters

In 1964, a few months after Lewis's death, *Letters to Malcolm: Chiefly on Prayer* came out, a book Lewis's publisher hailed as 'something of a present to a publisher'. An imaginary correspondence between the writer and Malcolm, a fictitious old friend, the book presents 'two ordinary laymen discussing the practical and speculative problems of prayer', as Lewis himself described it.

When I spoke of prayer without words I don't think I meant anything so exalted as what mystics call the 'prayer of silence'. And when I spoke of being 'at the top of one's form' I didn't mean it purely in a spiritual sense. The condition of the body comes in; for I suppose a man may be in a state of grace and yet very sleepy.

And, talking of sleepiness, I entirely agree with you that no one in his senses, if he has any power of ordering his own day, would reserve his chief prayers for bed-time – obviously the worst possible hour for any action which needs concentration. The trouble is that thousands of unfortunate people can hardly find any other. Even for us, who are the lucky ones, it is not always easy. My own plan, when hard pressed, is to seize any time, and place, however unsuitable, in preference to the last waking moment. On a day of travelling – with, perhaps, some ghastly meeting at the end of it – I'd rather pray sitting in a crowded train than put it off till midnight when one reaches a hotel bedroom with aching head and dry throat and one's mind partly in a stupor and partly in a whirl. On other, and slightly less crowded, days a bench in a park, or a back street where one can pace up and down, will do …

When one prays in strange places and at strange times one can't kneel, to be sure. I won't say this doesn't matter. The body ought to pray as well as the soul … Kneeling does matter, but other things matter even more. A concentrated mind and a sitting body make for better prayer than a kneeling body and a mind half asleep …

Why you find it so important to pray for people by their Christian names I can't imagine. I always assume God knows their surnames as well. I am afraid many people appear in my prayers only as 'that old man at Crewe' or 'the waitress' or even 'that man'. One may have lost, or may never have known, their names and yet remember how badly they need to be prayed for.

Letters to Malcolm: Chiefly on Prayer

The first radio talk in the series *What Christians Believe* went out on 11 January 1942, and later became Book II of *Mere Christianity*. Broadcast at a time when Britain was at war, with her young men and women away from home, and those very homes sometimes the targets of enemy bombs, this clear explanation of the Christian faith by 'a very ordinary layman' met a real need and brought in a huge correspondence, all of which Lewis answered himself.

The Christian is in a different position from other people who are trying to be good. They hope, by being good, to please God if there is one; or – if they think there is not – at least they hope to deserve approval from good men. But the Christian thinks any good he does comes from the Christ-life inside him. He does not think God will love us because we are good, but that God will make us good because He loves us; just as the roof of a greenhouse does not attract the sun because it is bright, but becomes bright because the sun shines on it.

And let me make it quite clear that when Christians say the Christ-life is in them, they do not mean simply something mental or moral. When they speak of being 'in Christ' or of Christ being 'in them', this is not simply a way of saying that they are thinking about Christ or copying Him. They mean that Christ is actually operating through them; that the whole mass of Christians are the physical organism through which Christ acts – that we are His fingers and muscles, the cells of His body. And perhaps that explains one or two things. It explains why this new life is spread not only by purely mental acts like belief, but by bodily acts like baptism and Holy Communion. It is not merely the spreading of an idea; it is more like evolution – a biological or super-biological fact. There is no good trying to be more spiritual than God. God never meant man to be a purely spiritual creature. That is why He uses material things like bread and wine to put the new life into us. We may think this rather crude and unspiritual. God does not: He invented eating. He likes matter. He invented it.

Here is another thing that used to puzzle me. Is it not frightfully unfair that this new life should be confined to people who have heard of Christ and been able to believe in Him? But the truth is God has not told us what His arrangements about the other people are. We do know that no man can be saved except through Christ; we do not know that only those who know Him can be saved through Him. But in the meantime, if you are worried about the people outside, the most unreasonable thing you can do is to remain outside yourself. Christians are Christ's body, the organism through which He works. Every addition to that body enables Him to do more. If you want to help those outside you must add your own little cell to the body of Christ who alone can help them. Cutting off a man's fingers would be an odd way of getting him to do more work …

I wonder whether people who ask God to interfere openly and directly in our world quite realize what it will be like when He does. When that happens, it is the end of the world. When the author walks on to the stage the play is over. God is going to invade, all right: but what is the good of saying you are on His side then, when you see the whole natural universe melting away like a dream and something else – something it never entered your head to conceive – comes crashing in; something so beautiful to some of us and so terrible to others that none of us will have any choice left? For this time it will be God without disguise; something so overwhelming that it will strike either irresistible love or irresistible horror into every creature. It will be too late then to choose your side. There is no use saying you choose to lie down when it has become impossible to stand up. That will not be the time for choosing: it will be the time when we discover which side we really have chosen, whether we realized it before or not. Now, today, this moment, is our chance to choose the right side. God is holding back to give us that chance. It will not last for ever. We must take it or leave it.

Mere Christianity

The Great Divorce, Lewis's allegory of Heaven and Hell, was published on 14 January 1946. In it the writer dreams that he is in a bus which plies between Heaven and Hell, together with a motley band of individuals such as one might meet at any bus stop, with all their annoying habits. The fantasy becomes a meditation upon good and evil, but is not meant 'to arouse factual curiosity about the details of the after-world'.

Blake wrote The Marriage of Heaven and Hell. *If I have written of their Divorce, this is not because I think myself a fit antagonist for so great a genius, nor even because I feel at all sure that I know what he meant. But in some sense or other the attempt to make that marriage is perennial. The attempt is based on the belief that reality never presents us with an absolutely unavoidable 'either or'; that, granted skill and patience and (above all) time enough, some way of embracing both alternatives can always be found; that mere development or adjustment or refinement will somehow turn evil into good without our being called on for a final and total rejection of anything we should like to retain. This belief I take to be a disastrous error. You cannot take all luggage with you on all journeys; on one journey even your right hand and your right eye may be among the things you have to leave behind. We are not living in a world where all roads are radii of a circle, and where all, if followed long enough, will therefore draw gradually nearer and finally meet at the centre: rather in a world where every road, after a few miles, forks into two, and each of those into two again, and at each fork you must make a decision. Even on the biological level life is not like a river but like a tree. It does not move towards unity but away from it, and the creatures grow further apart as they increase in perfection. Good, as it ripens, becomes continually more different not only from evil but from other good.*

I do not think that all who choose wrong roads perish; but their rescue consists in being put back on the right road. A wrong sum can be put right; but only by going back till you find the error and working it afresh from that point, never by simply going on. Evil can be undone, but it cannot 'develop' into good. Time does not heal it. The spell must be unwound, bit by bit, 'with backward mutters of disseevering power' – or else not. It is still 'either or'. If we insist on keeping Hell (or even earth) we shall not see Heaven: if we accept Heaven we shall not be able to retain even the smallest and most intimate souvenirs of Hell.

I believe, to be sure, that any man who reaches Heaven will find that what he abandoned (even in plucking out his right eye) has not been lost: that the kernel of what he was really seeking even in his most depraved wishes will be there, beyond expectation, waiting for him in 'the High Countries'. In that sense it will be true for those who have completed the journey (and for no others) to say that good is everything and Heaven everywhere. But we, at this end of the road, must not try to anticipate that retrospective vision. If we do, we are likely to embrace the false and disastrous converse, and fancy that everything is good and everywhere is Heaven.

But what, you ask, of earth? Earth, I think, will not be found by anyone to be in the end a very distinct place. I think earth, if chosen instead of Heaven, will turn out to have been, all along, only a region in Hell: and earth, if put second to Heaven, to have been from the beginning a part of Heaven itself.

The Great Divorce

February

FEBRUARY IS STILL VERY MUCH A WINTER month in England and, although the climate may be changing now, in Lewis's day it was indeed 'February fill-dyke', one of the rainiest times of the year. But there were signs of the coming spring, in that snowdrops and perhaps even a few early daffodils were brightening the landscape. Dedicated walkers like Lewis would have been out enjoying a brisk walk, returning home to the joys of a glowing fire in the study, the scene completed by a large pot of tea and hot buttered toast.

Lewis spent his winter months lecturing, seeing friends and writing. In February 1942 *The Screwtape Letters* was published. The book contains the imaginary correspondence between a senior devil and a junior, and in it we can all too easily recognize ourselves, as in the extract about the sanctimonious son praying for his difficult mother. 'But that's me! – How did he know?'

In February 1944 Lewis began his fourth series of BBC talks, *Beyond Personality*, still keeping his typically down-to-earth approach. One of his great gifts was the ability to handle a difficult subject in words and pictures that any untrained but sensible person could grasp.

One of the great themes in Jack Lewis's life was what he called 'Northernness', a manifestation of 'Joy' brought about by poetry – first by Longfellow's *Saga of King Olaf* and later by *Tegner's Drapa* and *Balder the Beautiful*. Early in 1912, in the schoolroom in Malvern, Jack's long winter was once more transformed, in a single moment, by some words and an illustration in a magazine.

My eye fell upon a headline and a picture, carelessly, expecting nothing. A moment later, as the poet says, 'The sky had turned round'.

What I had read was the words Siegfried and the Twilight of the Gods. *What I had seen was one of Arthur Rackham's illustrations to that volume. I had never heard of Wagner, nor of Siegfried. I thought the Twilight of the Gods meant the twilight in which the gods lived. How did I know, at once and beyond question, that this was no Celtic, or silvan, or terrestrial twilight? But so it was. Pure 'Northernness' engulfed me: a vision of huge, clear spaces hanging above the Atlantic in the endless twilight of Northern summer, remoteness, severity ... and almost at the same moment I knew that I had met this before, long, long ago (it hardly seems longer now) in* Tegner's Drapa, *that Siegfried (whatever it might be) belonged to the same world as Balder and the sunward-sailing cranes. And with that plunge back into my own past there arose at once, almost like heartbreak, the memory of Joy itself, the knowledge that I had once had what I had now lacked for years, that I was returning at last from exile and desert lands to my own country; and the distance of the Twilight of the Gods and the distance of my own past Joy, both unattainable, flowed together into a single, unendurable sense of desire and loss, which suddenly became one with the loss of the whole experience, which, as I now stared round that dusty schoolroom like a man recovering from unconsciousness, had already vanished, had eluded me at the very moment when I could first say* It is. *And at once I knew (with fatal knowledge) that to 'have it again' was the supreme and only important object of desire.*

After this everything played into my hands. One of my father's many presents to us boys had been a gramophone. Thus at the moment when my eyes fell on the words Siegfried and the Twilight of the Gods, *gramophone catalogues were already one of my favourite forms of reading; but I had never remotely dreamed that the records from Grand Opera with their queer German or Italian names could have anything to do with me. Nor did I for a week or two think so now. But then I was assailed from a new quarter. A magazine called* The Soundbox *was doing synopses of great operas week by week, and it now did the whole* Ring. *I read in a rapture and discovered who Siegfried was and what was the 'twilight' of the gods. I could contain myself no longer – I began a poem, a heroic poem on the Wagnerian version of the Niblung story. My only source was the abstracts in* The Soundbox, *and I was so ignorant that I made Alberich rhyme with* ditch *and Mime with* time. *My model was Pope's* Odyssey *and the poem began (with some mixture of mythologies)*

Descend to earth, descend, celestial Nine
And chant the ancient legends of the Rhine …

Since the fourth book had carried me only as far as the last scene of The Rheingold, *the reader will not be surprised to hear that the poem was never finished. But it was not a waste of time, and I can still see just what it did for me and where it began to do it … All this time I had still not heard a note of Wagner's music, though the very shape of the printed letters of his name had become to me a magical symbol. Next holidays, in the dark, crowded shop of T. Edens Osborne (on whom be peace), I first heard a record of* The Ride of the Valkyries … *To a boy already crazed with 'the Northernness', whose higher musical experience had been Sullivan,* The Ride *came like a thunderbolt. From that moment Wagnerian records … became the chief drain on my pocket money and the presents I invariably asked for …*

That summer our cousin H. … asked us to spend some weeks with her … There, on her drawing room table, I found the very book which had started the whole affair and which I had never dared to hope I should see … I have seldom coveted anything as I coveted that book; and when I heard that there was a cheaper edition … I knew I could never rest until it was mine. I got it in the end.

Surprised by Joy

The Screwtape Letters were first published as a book in February 1942 and are a series of letters written by Screwtape, a senior devil in Hell's civil service, to Wormwood, a younger devil, with the purpose of helping Wormwood to capture the soul of a 'patient'. The letters show what a human life looks like from the viewpoint of Hell, and how seemingly insignificant choices in everyday life can have immortal consequences. In his Preface Lewis wrote:

There are two equal and opposite errors into which our race can fall about the devils. One is to disbelieve in their existence. The other is to believe, and to feel an excessive and unhealthy interest in them. They themselves are equally pleased by both errors and hail a materialist or a magician with the same delight …

Readers are advised to remember that the devil is a liar. Not everything that Screwtape says should be assumed to be true even from his own angle. I have made no attempt to identify any of the human beings mentioned in the letters; but I think it very unlikely that the portraits, say, of Father Spike or the patient's mother, are wholly just. There is wishful thinking in Hell as well as on Earth.

And here is Screwtape writing to Wormwood, with advice on handling his patient's behaviour to his mother:

It is, no doubt, impossible to prevent his praying for his mother, but we have ways of rendering the prayers innocuous. Make sure that they are always very 'spiritual', that he is always concerned with the state of her soul and never with her rheumatism. Two advantages will follow. In the first place, his attention will be kept on what he regards as her sins, by which with a little guidance from you, he can be induced to mean any of her actions which are inconvenient or irritating to himself. Thus you can keep rubbing the wounds of the day a little sorer even while he is on his knees; the operation is not at all difficult and you will find it very entertaining. In the second place, since his ideas about her soul will be very crude and often erroneous, he will, in some degree, be praying for an imaginary person, and it will be your task to make that imaginary person daily less and less like the real mother – the sharp-tongued old lady at the breakfast table. In time, you may get the cleavage so wide that no thought or feeling from his prayers for the imagined mother will ever flow over into his treatment of the real one. I have had patients of my own so well in hand that they could be turned at a moment's notice from impassioned prayer for a wife's or son's 'soul' to beating or insulting the real wife or son without a qualm.

When two humans have lived together for many years it usually happens that each has tones of voice and expressions of face which are almost unendurably irritating to the other. Work on that. Bring fully into the consciousness of your patient that particular lift of his mother's eyebrows which he learned to dislike in the nursery, and let him think how much he dislikes it. Let him assume that she knows how annoying it is and does it to annoy — if you know your job he will not notice the immense improbability of the assumption. And, of course, never let him suspect that he has tones and looks which similarly annoy her. As he cannot see or hear himself, this is easily managed.

In civilized life domestic hatred usually expresses itself by saying things which would appear quite harmless on paper (the words *are not offensive) but in such a voice, or at such a moment, that they are not far short of a blow in the face. To keep this up you and Glubose must see to it that each of these two fools has a sort of double standard. Your patient must demand that all his own utterances are to be taken at their face value and judged simply on the actual words, while at the same time judging all his mother's utterances with the fullest and most over-sensitive interpretation of the tone and the context and the suspected intention. She must be encouraged to do the same to him. Hence from every quarrel they can both go away convinced, or very nearly convinced, that they are quite innocent.*

The Screwtape Letters

Having started his radio talks in January 1942, by February 1944 Lewis was into his fourth series for the BBC, *Beyond Personality*, which became Book IV of *Mere Christianity*, with the subtitle 'Or first steps in the doctrine of the Trinity'. The most theological of the broadcast series, *Beyond Personality* dealt with such topics as the Trinity, Time, the Incarnation and why Christians aren't necessarily nicer people than non-Christians.

In a way I quite understand why some people are put off by theology. I remember once when I had been giving a talk to the RAF [Royal Air Force], an old, hard-bitten officer got up and said, 'I've no use for all that stuff. But, mind you, I'm a religious man too. I know there's a God. I've felt Him: out alone in the desert at night: the tremendous mystery. And that's just why I don't believe all your neat little dogmas and formulas about Him. To anyone who's met the real thing they all seem so petty and pedantic and unreal!'

Now in a sense I quite agreed with that man. I think he has probably had a real experience of God in the desert. And when he turned from that experience to the Christian creeds, I think he really was turning from something real to something less real. In the same way, if a man has once looked at the Atlantic from the beach, and then goes and looks at a map of the Atlantic, he also will be turning from something real to something less real: turning from real waves to a bit of coloured paper. But here comes the point. The map is admittedly only coloured paper, but there are two things you have to remember about it. In the first place, it is based on what hundreds and thousands of people have found out by sailing the real Atlantic. In that way it has behind it masses of experience just as real as the one you could have from the beach; only, while yours would be a single glimpse, the map fits all those different experiences together. In the second place, if you want to go anywhere, the map is absolutely necessary. As long as you are content with walks on the beach, your own glimpses are far more fun than looking at a map. But the map is going to be more use than walks on the beach if you want to get to America.

Now, theology is like the map. Merely learning and thinking about the Christian doctrines, if you stop there, is less real and less exciting than the sort of thing my friend got in the desert. Doctrines are not God: they are only a kind of map. But that map is based on the experience of hundreds of people who really were in touch with God – experiences compared with

which any thrills or pious feelings you and I are likely to get on our own are very elementary and very confused. And second-
ly, if you want to get any further, you must use the map. You see, what happened to that man in the desert may have been
real, and was certainly exciting, but nothing comes of it. It leads nowhere. There is nothing to do about it. In fact, that is just
why a vague religion – all about feeling God in nature, and so on – is so attractive. It is all thrills and no work; like watch-
ing the waves from the beach. But you will not get to Newfoundland by studying the Atlantic that way, and you will not get
eternal life by simply feeling the presence of God in flowers or music. Neither will you get anywhere by looking at maps with-
out going to sea. Nor will you be very safe if you go to sea without a map.

In other words, theology is practical: especially now. In the old days, when there was less education and discussion, per-
haps it was possible to get on with a very few simple ideas about God. But it is not so now. Everyone reads, everyone hears
things discussed. Consequently, if you do not listen to theology, that will not mean that you have no ideas about God. It will
mean that you have a lot of wrong ones – bad, muddled, out-of-date ideas. For a great many of the ideas about God which
are trotted out as novelties today are simply the ones which real theologians tried centuries ago and rejected. To believe in the
popular religion of modern England is retrogression – like believing the earth is flat.

'Beyond Personality' in Mere Christianity

When Lewis first went back to Oxford after the Great War he expected to become a philosopher. Although not then a Christian, he was convinced that there was an 'Absolute' and that morals were of true value. In 1943, by then a firm Christian, Lewis developed this earlier thinking in three Riddell Memorial Lectures for the University of Durham, later published as *The Abolition of Man* and hailed as a masterpiece of clear thinking.

St Augustine defines virtue as ordo amoris, *the ordinate condition of the affections in which every object is accorded that kind and degree of love which is appropriate to it. Aristotle says that the aim of education is to make the pupil like and dislike what he ought. When the age for reflective thought comes, the pupil who has been thus trained in 'ordinate affections' or 'just sentiments' will easily find the first principles in Ethics; but to the corrupt man they will never be visible at all and he can make no progress in that science. Plato before him had said the same. The little human animal will not at first have the right responses. It must be trained to feel pleasure, liking, disgust, and hatred at those things which really are pleasant, likeable, disgusting and hateful. In the* Republic, *the well-nurtured youth is one 'who would see most clearly whatever was amiss in ill-made works of man or ill-grown works of nature … All this before he is of an age to reason; so that when Reason at length comes to him, then, bred as he has been, he will hold out his hands in welcome and recognize her because of the affinity he bears to her' … The Chinese also speak of a great thing (the greatest thing) called the* Tao. *It is the reality beyond all predicates, the abyss that was before the Creator Himself. It is Nature, it is the Way, the Road. It is the way in which the universe goes on, the Way in which things everlastingly emerge, stilly and tranquilly, into space and time. It is also the Way which every man should tread in imitation of that cosmic and supercosmic progression, conforming all activities to that great exemplar … The ancient Jews likewise praise the Law as being 'true' …*

It is the doctrine of objective value, the belief that certain attitudes are really true, and others really false, to the kind of thing the universe is and the kind of things we are.

The Abolition of Man

Lewis thought that if contemporary Christians were to believe fully in Jesus Christ, they also needed to believe fully in His return or Second Coming, as their ancestors had done. In 'The World's Last Night' (originally published under the title 'Christian Hope – Its Meaning for Today' in the Winter 1951–2 issue of *Religion in Life*) he dealt with the various thoughts that might prevent people from giving due weight to this important but difficult doctrine.

'Hereafter,' said Our Lord Himself, 'shall ye see the Son of Man … coming in the clouds of heaven.' If this is not an integral part of the faith once given to the saints, I do not know what is …

The doctrine of the second coming teaches us that we do not and cannot know when the world drama will end. The curtain may be rung down at any moment: say, before you have finished reading this paragraph. This seems to some people intolerably frustrating. So many things would be interrupted. Perhaps you were going to get married next month, perhaps you were going to get a raise next week: you may be on the verge of a great scientific discovery; you may be maturing great social and political reforms. Surely no good and wise God would be so very unreasonable as to cut all this short? Not now, *of all moments!*

But we think thus because we keep on assuming that we know the play. We do not know the play. We do not even know whether we are in Act I or Act V. We do not know who are the major and who the minor characters. The Author knows. The audience, if there is an audience (if angels and archangels and all the company of heaven fill the pit and the stalls), may have an inkling. But we, never seeing the play from the outside, never meeting any characters except the tiny minority who are 'on' in the same scenes as ourselves, wholly ignorant of the future and very imperfectly informed about the past, cannot tell at what moment the end ought to come. That it will come when it ought, we may be sure; but we waste our time in guessing when that will be. That it has a meaning we may be sure, but we cannot see it. When it is over, we may be told. We are led to expect that the Author will have something to say to each of us on the part that each of us has played. The playing it well is what matters infinitely.

'The World's Last Night' in Fern-seed and Elephants

March

MARCH IS STILL JUST WITHIN WINTER, but all the signs of spring are there – lighter days, softer winds, daffodils aplenty and that general feeling that life is going to burst out anew and is really going to 'spring'. The bare branches of trees have a faint dusting of green with the promise of new leaves, birds are busy gathering twigs and soft things for their nests, gardens generally are stirring into new life, and Easter is either here or due very shortly.

Spring is also traditionally a time for poets, and in March 1919 Lewis's first book of poetry, *Spirits in Bondage – A Cycle of Lyrics*, was published, when he was only 20 years old. In March 1960 came one of his most seminal religious books, *The Four Loves*.

Perhaps most importantly for him, it was in March 1957 that he and Joy Davidman, then in hospital, were married in a religious ceremony, and so began the real marriage that was to bring them both so much happiness.

In 1913 Lewis was at school in Malvern ('Wyvern' in his diaries). There, he says, he became a prig, a high brow, and also, under the influence of a young and dressy schoolmaster, flashy. However, more importantly, he was more influenced by another master, known as Smewgy. Though his face seemed to resemble that of a frog, Smewgy had the voice of an angel and the gift of making poetry soar.

There were two blessings at Wyvern that wore no disguise: one of them was my form master, Smewgy as we called him. I spell the name so as to ensure the right pronunciation – the first syllable should rhyme exactly with fugue *– though the Wyvernian spelling was 'Smugy'.*

Except at Oldie's I had been fortunate in my teachers ever since I was born; but Smewgy was 'beyond expectation, beyond hope'. He was a grey-head with large spectacles and a wide mouth which combined to give him a froglike expression, but nothing could be less froglike than his voice. He was honey-tongued. Every verse he read turned into music on his lips: something midway between speech and song. It is not the only good way of reading verse, but it is the way to enchant boys; more dramatic and less rhythmical ways can be learned later. He first taught me the right sensuality of poetry, how it should be savoured and mouthed in solitude. Of Milton's 'Thrones, Dominations, Princedoms, Virtues, Powers' he said, 'That line made me happy for a week.' It was not the sort of thing I had heard anyone say before.

Nor had I ever met before perfect courtesy in a teacher. It had nothing to do with softness; Smewgy could be very severe, but it was the severity of a judge, weighty and measured, without taunting –

He never yet no vileinye ne sayde
In all his lyf unto no maner wight.

He had a difficult team to drive, for our form consisted partly of youngsters, New Bugs with scholarships, starting there like myself, and partly of veterans who had arrived there at the end of their slow journey up the school …

Even had he taught us nothing else, to be in Smewgy's form was to be in a measure ennobled. Amidst all the banal ambition and flashy splendours of school life he stood as a permanent reminder of things more gracious, more humane, larger and cooler ... He could enchant but he could also analyse. An idiom or a textual crux, once expounded by Smewgy, became clear as day. He made us feel that the scholar's demand for accuracy was not merely pedantic, still less an arbitrary moral discipline, but rather a niceness, a delicacy, to lack which argued 'a gross and swainish disposition'. I began to see that the reader who misses syntactical points in a poem is missing aesthetic points as well ...

Smewgy taught us Latin and Greek, but everything else came in incidentally. The books I liked best under his teaching were Horace's Odes, Aeneid IV, *and Euripides'* Bacchae. *I had always in one sense 'liked' my classical work, but hitherto this had only been the pleasure that everyone feels in mastering a craft. Now I tasted the classics as poetry ... Here was something very different from the Northernness ... A new quality entered my imagination: something Mediterranean and volcanic, the orgiastic drum-beat ...*

The other undisguised blessing of the Coll was 'the Gurney', the school library ... In the Gurney I found Corpus Poeticum Boreale *and tried, vainly but happily, to hammer out the originals from the translation at the bottom of the page. There too I found Milton, Yeats, and a book on Celtic mythology, which soon became, if not a rival, yet a humble companion, to Norse. That did me good; to enjoy two mythologies (or three, now that I had begun to love the Greek), fully aware of their differing flavours, is a balancing thing, and makes for catholicity. I felt keenly the difference between the stony and fiery sublimity of Asgard, the green, leafy, amorous, and elusive world of Cruachan and the Red Branch and Tir-nan-Og, the harder, more defiant, sun-bright beauty of Olympus. I began (presumably in the holidays) an epic on Cuchulain and another on Finn, in English hexameters and in fourteeners respectively. Luckily they were abandoned before these easy and vulgar metres had time to spoil my ear.*

Surprised by Joy

Lewis's first ambition was to be a poet, an ambition roused and stimulated during his stay with W.T. Kirkpatrick in Bookham, Surrey. During his first holiday at home, in 1915, he wrote two of the poems that were to appear in his first book, *Spirits in Bondage – A Cycle of Lyrics*. Other pieces in the book were written at Oxford, in France and back in England. The book was published in 1919, when Lewis was still only 20. Today it can be read in full in the collection, *Poems*.

They hate my world! Then let that other God
Come from the outer spaces glory-shod,
And from this castle I have built on Night
Steal forth my own thought's children into light,
If such an one there be. But far away
He walks the airy fields of endless day,
And my rebellious sons have called Him long
And vainly called. My order still is strong
And like to me nor second none I know.
Whither the mammoth went this creature too shall go.
           From 'Satan Speaks' in Spirits in Bondage

Then suddenly, again, the room,
Familiar books about me piled,
And I alone amid the gloom,
By one more mocking dream beguiled.

And still no nearer to the Light,
And still no further from myself,
Alone and lost in clinging night
– (The clock's still ticking on the shelf).

Then do I envy solid folk
Who sit of evenings by the fire,
After their work and doze and smoke,
And are not fretted by desire.

   From 'In Praise of Solid People' in Spirits in Bondage

Jack Lewis loved being in Oxford, especially because of the opportunities that it gave him to read virtually any book he chose. In this letter of March 1928 he tried to tell his father, Albert (who was still supporting him financially), something of his life there.

I spend all my mornings in the Bodleian … If only you could smoke, and if only there were upholstered chairs, the Bodleian would be one of the most delightful places in the world. I sit in 'Duke Humphrey's Library', the oldest part, a fifteenth-century building with a very beautiful painted wooden ceiling above me and a little mullioned window at my left hand through which I look down on the garden of Exeter [College] where, these mornings, I see the sudden squalls of wind and rain driving the first blossoms off the fruit trees and snowing the lawn with them …

The library itself – I mean the books – is mostly in a labyrinth of cellars under the neighbouring squares. This room however is full of books (duplicate copies I suppose, or overflows) which stand in little cases at right angles to the wall, so that between each pair there is a kind of little 'box' – in the public-house sense of the word – and in these boxes one sits and reads. By a merciful provision, however many books you may send for, they will all be left on your chosen table at night for you to resume work next morning: so that one gradually accumulates a pile as comfortably as in one's own room. There is not, as in modern libraries, a forbidding framed notice to shriek 'Silence'; on the contrary, a more modest request: 'Talk little and tread lightly'. There is indeed always a faint murmur going on of semi-whispered conversations in neighbouring boxes. It disturbs no one. I rather like to hear the hum of the hive, and it is pleasant when someone steps into your box and says, 'Hello, are you here?'

Letters

Lewis's writings were becoming known in America, and in 1958, in response to a request from Atlanta, Georgia, he wrote and recorded *Four Talks on Love*, subsequently using them as the basis for one of his best-known books, *The Four Loves*, which was published in March 1960. The four kinds of love are **Affection** (in Greek *Storge*), **Friendship** (*Philia*), **Eros** *(Eros)* and **Charity** (*Agape*).

I begin with the humblest and most widely diffused of loves, the love in which our experience seems to differ least from that of the animals. Let me add at once that I do not on that account give it a lower value. Nothing in Man is either worse or better for being shared with the beasts. When we blame a man for being 'a mere animal', we mean not that he displays animal characteristics (we all do) but that he displays these, and only these, on occasions where the specifically human was demanded …

The Greeks call this love storge *(two syllables and the g is hard). I shall here call it simply **Affection**. My Greek lexicon defines* storge *as 'affection, especially of parents to offspring'; but also of offspring to parents. And that, I have no doubt, is the original form of the thing as well as the central meaning of the word. The image we must start with is that of a mother nursing a baby, a bitch or a cat with a basketful of puppies or kittens; all in a squeaking, nuzzling heap together; purrings, lickings, baby-talk, milk, warmth, the smell of young life …*

*When either Affection or Eros is one's theme, one finds a prepared audience. The importance and beauty of both have been stressed and almost exaggerated again and again … But very few modern people think **Friendship** a love of comparable value or even a love at all. I cannot remember that any poem since* In Memoriam, *or any novel, has celebrated it. Tristan and Isolde, Antony and Cleopatra, Romeo and Juliet, have innumerable counterparts in modern literature: David and Jonathan, Pylades and Orestes, Roland and Oliver, Amis and Amile, have not. To the Ancients, Friendship seemed the happiest and most fully human of all loves; the crown of life and the school of virtue. The modern world, in comparison, ignores it. We admit of course that besides a wife and family a man needs a few 'friends'. But the very tone of the admission, and the sort of acquaintanceships which those who make it would describe as 'friendships', show clearly that what they are talking about has very little to do with that* philia *which Aristotle classified among the virtues, or that* Amicitia *on which*

Cicero wrote a book. It is something quite marginal; not a main course in life's banquet; a diversion; something that fills up the chinks of one's time …

*By **Eros** I mean of course that state which we call 'being in love'; or, if you prefer, that kind of love which lovers are 'in' … In an earlier chapter I described Affection as the love in which our experience seems to come closest to that of the animals. Surely, it might be asked, our sexual functions bring us equally close? This is quite true as regards human sexuality in general. But … I am enquiring not into the sexuality which is common to us and the beasts or even common to all men, but into one uniquely human variation of it which develops within 'love' – what I call Eros. The carnal or animally sexual element within Eros, I intend (following an old usage) to call Venus … My treatment rules out mere sexuality – sexuality without Eros – on grounds that have nothing to do with morals; because it is irrelevant to our purpose …*

William Morris wrote a poem called Love is Enough *and someone is said to have reviewed it briefly in the words 'It isn't' … The natural loves are not self-sufficient. Something else, at first vaguely described as 'decency and common sense', but later revealed as goodness, and finally as the whole Christian life in one particular relation, must come to the help of the mere feeling if the feeling is to be kept sweet …*

*God is love … He communicates to men a share of His own Gift-love … Divine Gift-love – Love Himself working in a man – is wholly disinterested and desires what is simply best for the beloved … 'Our wills are ours to make them Thine.' And as all Christians know, there is another way of giving to God: every stranger whom we feed or clothe is Christ. And this apparently is Gift-love to God whether we know it or not … That such a Gift-love comes by Grace and should be called **Charity**, everyone will agree.*

The Four Loves

As Jack had not been happy at school in England or Belfast, in 1914, aged 15, he was sent to Great Bookham in Surrey to be 'crammed' for Oxford by W.T. Kirkpatrick, a retired teacher who had been Jack's father's headmaster. This was one of the most formative periods of the young Jack's life, for apart from the academic learning, Mr Kirkpatrick taught him how to use his time to the full, with a daily schedule which Lewis greatly enjoyed.

We now settled into a routine which has ever since served in my mind as an archetype, so that what I still mean when I speak of a 'normal' day (and lament that normal days are so rare) is a day of the Bookham pattern. For if I could please myself I would always live as I lived there. I would choose always to breakfast at exactly eight and to be at my desk by nine, there to read or write till one. If a cup of good tea or coffee could be brought me about eleven, so much the better. A step or so out of doors for a pint of beer would not do quite so well; for a man does not want to drink alone and if you meet a friend in the tap-room the break is likely to be extended beyond its ten minutes. At one precisely lunch should be on the table; and by two at the latest I would be on the road. Not, except at rare intervals, with a friend. Walking and talking are two very great pleasures, but it is a mistake to combine them. Our own noise blots out the sounds and silences of the outdoor world; and talking leads almost inevitably to smoking, and then farewell to nature as far as one of our senses is concerned. The only friend to walk with is one (such as I found, during the holidays, in Arthur) who so exactly shares your taste for each mood of the countryside that a glance, a halt, or at most a nudge, is enough to assure us that the pleasure is shared. The return from the walk, and the arrival of tea, should be exactly coincident, and not later than a quarter past four. Tea should be taken in solitude … For eating and reading are two pleasures that combine admirably … At five a man should be at work again, and at it till seven. Then, at the evening meal and after, comes the time for talk, or, failing that, for lighter reading; and unless you are making a night of it with your cronies … there is no reason why you should ever be in bed later than eleven.

Surprised by Joy

Jack Lewis and his brother Warnie were always regarded as confirmed bachelors, enjoying the predominantly male atmosphere of university life in Oxford. In 1956, however, in order to allow an American friend, Joy Davidman Gresham, and her two sons to stay legally in England, Jack married Joy in a Registry Office ceremony. They kept separate establishments until March 1957, when they were married in a religious ceremony in the Wingfield-Morris Hospital, Oxford. Here is an extract from a letter that Jack wrote at the time:

Yes, it is true. I married (knowingly) a very sick, save by near-miracle a dying, woman. She is the Joy Davidman whose Smoke on the Mountain *I think you read. She is in the Wingfield Morris Hospital at Headington. When I see her each weekend she is, to a layman's eyes (but not to a doctor's knowledge) in full convalescence, better every week. The disease is of course cancer: by which I lost my mother, my father, and my favourite aunt. She knows her own state of course: I would allow no lies to be told to a grown-up and a Christian. As you can imagine, new beauty and new tragedy have entered my life. You would be surprised (or perhaps you would not?) to know how much of a strange sort of happiness and even gaiety there is between us …*

    I don't doubt that Joy and I (and David and Douglas, the two boys) will have your prayers. Douglas is an absolute charmer (11 ½). David, at first sight less engaging, is at any rate a comically appropriate stepson for me (13), being almost exactly what I was – bookworm, pedant, and a bit of a prig …

In another letter Jack said:

I am newly married and to a dying woman. Every moment is spent at her bedside. I am sure we may both count on your prayers: and I, your prayers for help and guidance in the difficult responsibility of bringing up two orphan stepsons. I have only one quali-fication, if it is one: these two boys are now facing the very same calamity that befell my brother and me at about their age.

Letters

April

WITH APRIL SPRING REALLY HAS ARRIVED. The hours of daylight are longer, the light itself is stronger, and people begin to think of getting out of doors, of gardens, of walking in the good, fresh air, even of another new start as summer beckons.

In April 1905, when Jack was six, the Lewis family moved to the 'New House' – 'Little Lea', with its view over Belfast Lough to the front, and the Holywood Hills behind – countryside which was to encourage a romantic bent in Lewis as he grew up there, and which helped nourish his lifelong love of walking.

In April 1922 Jack began his long epic poem *Dymer*, and in April 1943 *Christian Behaviour*, which was to form another part of *Mere Christianity*, was published.

In April 1960 Lewis and Joy spent an idyllic holiday in Greece. Despite her illness, Joy found an amazing strength, 'as if she were divinely supported'.

Jack Lewis spent the first years of his life in Dundela Villas in Belfast, but when he was six the family moved into a larger, detached house further out in the country. Called 'Little Lea', it was generally referred to by the family as the 'New House', and here Jack – with his elder brother away at boarding school in England – developed a life of his own.

In 1905, my seventh year, the first great change in my life took place. We moved house. My father, growing, I suppose, in prosperity, decided to leave the semi-detached villa in which I had been born and build himself a much larger house, further out into what was then the country. The 'New House', as we continued for years to call it, was a large one even by my present standards; to a child it seemed less like a house than a city. My father, who had more capacity for being cheated than any man I have ever known, was badly cheated by his builders; the drains were wrong, the chimneys were wrong, and there was a draught in every room. None of this, however, mattered to a child. To me, the important thing about the move was that the background to my life became larger. The New House is almost a major character in my story. I am a product of long corridors, empty sunlit rooms, upstairs indoor silences, attics explored in solitude, distant noises of gurgling cisterns and pipes, and the noise of wind under the tiles. Also, of endless books. My father bought all the books he read and never got rid of any of them. There were books in the study, books in the drawing room, books in the cloakroom, books (two deep) in the great bookcase on the landing, books in a bedroom, books piled as high as my shoulder in the cistern attic, books of all kinds reflecting every transient stage of my parents' interests, books readable and unreadable, books suitable for a child and books most emphatically not. Nothing was forbidden me. In the seemingly endless rainy afternoons I took volume after volume from the shelves. I had always the same certainty of finding a book that was new to me as a man who walks into a field has of finding a new blade of grass. Where all these books had been before we came to the New House is a problem that never occurred to me until I began writing this paragraph. I have no idea of the answer.

Out of doors was 'the view' for which, no doubt, the site had been principally chosen. From our front door we looked down over wide fields to Belfast Lough and Hill. This was in the far-off days when Britain was the world's carrier and the

April

Lough was full of shipping; a delight to both us boys, but most to my brother. The sound of a steamer's horn at night still con-jures up my whole boyhood. Behind the house, greener, lower, and nearer than the Antrim mountains, were the Holywood Hills, but it was not till much later that they won my attention. The north-western prospect was what mattered at first; the interminable summer sunsets behind the blue ridges, and the rooks flying home …

The country I grew up in had everything to encourage a romantic bent, had indeed done so ever since I first looked at the unattainable Green Hills through the nursery window … My main haunt was the Holywood Hills … It is, by southern English standards, bleak. The woods, for we have a few, are of small trees, rowan and birch and small fir. The fields are small, divided by ditches with ragged sea-nipped hedges on top of them. There is a good deal of gorse and many outcroppings of rock. Small abandoned quarries, filled with cold-looking water, are surprisingly numerous. There is nearly always a wind whistling through the grass. Where you see a man ploughing there will be gulls following him and pecking at the furrow. There are no field-paths or rights of way, but that does not matter for everyone knows you – or if they do not know you, they know your kind and understand that you will shut gates and not walk over crops … The grass is soft, rich, and sweet, and the cottages, always whitewashed and single-storeyed and roofed with blue slate, light up the whole landscape.

Surprised by Joy

The four series of radio talks which Lewis did for the BBC each appeared as separate books before their final publication together in *Mere Christianity*, and in April 1943 one of these books, *Christian Behaviour*, was published. As the original talks had to fit into ten-minute slots, the material was expanded for the books, and in the case of *Christian Behaviour* Lewis wrote four extra chapters.

The first thing to get clear about Christian morality between man and man is that in this department Christ did not come to preach any brand-new morality. The Golden Rule of the New Testament (Do as you would be done by) is a summing up of what everyone, at bottom, had always known to be right. Really great moral teachers never do introduce new moralities: it is quacks and cranks who do that. As Dr Johnson said, 'People need to be reminded more often than they need to be instructed.' The real job of every moral teacher is to keep on bringing us back, time after time, to the old simple principles which we are all so anxious not to see; like bringing a horse back and back to the fence it has refused to jump or bringing a child back and back to the bit in its lesson that it wants to shirk.

The second thing to get clear is that Christianity has not, and does not profess to have, a detailed political programme for applying 'Do as you would be done by' to a particular society at a particular moment. It could not have. It is meant for all men at all times, and the particular programme which suited one place or time would not suit another. And, anyhow, that is not how Christianity works. When it tells you to feed the hungry it does not give you lessons in cookery. When it tells you to read the Scriptures it does not give you lessons in Hebrew and Greek, or even in English grammar. It was never intended to replace or supersede the ordinary human arts and sciences: it is rather a director which will set them all to the right jobs, and a source of energy which will give them all new life, if only they will put themselves at its disposal …

The New Testament, without going into details, gives us a pretty clear hint of what a fully Christian society would be like. Perhaps it gives us more than we can take. It tells us that there are to be no passengers or parasites: if man does not work, he ought not to eat. Everyone is to work with his own hands, and what is more, everyone's work is to produce something good: there will be no manufacture of silly luxuries and then of sillier advertisements to persuade us to buy them. And there is to be no 'swank' or 'side', no putting on airs. To that extent a Christian society would be what we now call Leftist. On the other hand, it is always insisting on obedience – obedience (and outward marks of respect) from all of us to properly appointed magistrates, from children to parents, and (I am afraid this is going to be very unpopular) from wives to husbands. Thirdly, it is to be a cheerful society: full of singing and rejoicing, and regarding worry or anxiety as wrong. Courtesy is one of the Christian virtues; and the New Testament hates what it calls 'busybodies'.

If there were such a society in existence and you or I visited it … each of us would like some bits of it, but I am afraid very few of us would like the whole thing … You will find this again and again about anything that is really Christian: everyone is attracted by bits of it and wants to pick out those bits and leave the rest. That is why … people who are fighting for quite opposite things can both say they are fighting for Christianity …

A Christian society is not going to arrive until most of us really want it: and we are not going to want it until we become fully Christian. I may repeat 'Do as you would be done by' till I am black in the face, but I cannot really carry it out till I love my neighbour as myself: and I cannot learn to love my neighbour as myself till I learn to love God: and I cannot learn to love God except by learning to obey Him.

And so, as I warned you, we are driven on to something more inward – driven on from social matters to religious matters. For the longest way round is the shortest way home.

'Christian Behaviour' in Mere Christianity

Jack Lewis had the gift of writing good letters to children, and kept up a voluminous correspondence with many once *The Lion, the Witch and the Wardrobe*, the first volume of *The Chronicles of Narnia*, was published in 1950. Before that few of his correspondents were children, but one exception was Sarah, the daughter of a former pupil, and his own godchild. In 1949 he wrote to her at the time of her confirmation, having not seen her for several years.

I am sorry to say that I don't think I shall be able to be at your confirmation on Saturday … If I had come and we had met, I am afraid you might have found me very shy and dull. (By the way, always remember that old people can be quite as shy with young people as young people can be with old. This explains what must seem to you the idiotic way in which so many grown-ups talk to you.) But I will try to do what I can by a letter. I think of myself as having to be two people for you. (1) The real, serious, Christian godfather. (2) The fairy godfather. As regards (2), I enclose a bit of the only kind of magic (a very dull kind) which I can work. Your mother will know how to deal with the spell. I think it will mean one or two, or even five, pounds for you now, *to get things you want, and the rest in the Bank for future use. As I say, it is a dull kind of magic and a really good godfather (of type 2) would do something much more interesting: but it is the best an old bachelor can think of, and it is with my love.*

　　As for No. 1, the serious Christian godfather, I feel very unfit for the work – just as you, I dare say, may feel very unfit for being confirmed and for receiving the Holy Communion. But then an angel would not be really fit and we must all do the best we can. So I suppose I must try to give you advice. And the bit of advice that comes into my head is this: don't expect (I mean, don't count on *and don't* demand*) that when you are confirmed, or when you make your first Communion, you will have all the* feelings *you would like to have. You may, of course: but also you may not. But don't worry if you don't get them. They aren't what matter. The things that are happening to you are quite real things whether you feel as you would wish or not, just as a meal will do a hungry person good even if he has a cold in the head which will rather spoil the taste. Our Lord will give us right* feelings *if He wishes – and then we must say Thank you. If He doesn't, then we must say to ourselves (and Him) that He knows us best. This, by the way, is one of the very few subjects on which I feel I do know* *something. For years after I had become a regular communicant I can't tell you how dull my feelings were and how my attention wandered at the most important moments. It is only in the last year or two that things have begun to come right – which just shows how important it is to keep on doing what you are told.*

Oh – I'd nearly forgotten – I have one *other piece of advice. Remember that there are only three kinds of things anyone need ever do. (1) Things we* ought *to do. (2) Things we've* got *to do. (3) Things we* like *doing. I say this because some people seem to spend so much of their time doing things for none of the three reasons, things like reading books they don't like because other people read them. Things you ought to do are things like doing one's school work or being nice to people. Things one has got to do are things like dressing and undressing, or household shopping. Things one likes doing – but of course I don't know what* you *like. Perhaps you'll write and tell me one day.*

Of course I always mention you in my prayers and will most especially on Saturday. Do the same for me.

Your affectionate godfather,

C.S. Lewis

Letters to Children

Lewis first conceived the story of 'Dymer' when he was 17. Dymer fathers a monster who finally becomes a god, having first killed Dymer. That early prose version was replaced by a long allegorical poem which Lewis began writing in April 1922. The poem, as he noted, 'found some good reviews and almost no readers'. Here are some of the earlier lines.

At Dymer's birth no comets scared the nation,
The public creche engulfed him with the rest,
And twenty separate Boards of Education
Closed round him. He was passed through every test,
Was vaccinated, numbered, washed and dressed,
Proctored, inspected, whipt, examined weekly
And for some nineteen years he bore it meekly.

For nineteen years they worked upon his soul,
Refining, chipping, moulding and adorning,
Then came the moment that undid the whole –
The ripple of rude life without a warning …

He lingered – Looking up, he saw ahead
The black and bristling frontage of a wood,
And over it the large sky swimming red,
Freckled with homeward crows. Surprised he stood
To feel that wideness quenching his hot mood,
Then shouted, 'Trembling darkness, trembling green,
What do you mean, wild wood, what do you mean?'

Dymer *in* Narrative Poems

Jack and Joy had married in March 1957 when she was seriously ill with cancer. A month later she left hospital and moved to The Kilns, Jack and Warnie's home. There she grew stronger, until in June 1958 her cancer was diagnosed as arrested. But 15 months later it returned, so in April 1960, to fulfil a lifetime's ambition, Jack and Joy had a holiday in Greece, together with Jack's long-time friends, Roger and June Lancelyn Green. Afterwards Jack wrote to a friend:

It looked very doubtful if Joy and I would be able to do our trip to Greece, but we did. From one point of view it was madness, but neither of us regrets it. She performed prodigies of strength, limping to the top of the Acropolis and up through the Lion gate of Mycenae and all about the medieval city of Rhodes. (Rhodes is simply the Earthly Paradise.) It was as if she were divinely supported. She came back in a nunc dimittis *frame of mind, having realized, beyond hope, her greatest, lifelong, this-worldly desire.*

There was a heavy price to pay in increased lameness and leg pains; not that her exertions had or could have any effect on the course of the cancers, but that the muscles etc. had been overtaxed …

I had some ado to prevent Joy (and myself) from relapsing into Paganism in Attica! At Daphne it was hard not to pray to Apollo the Healer. But somehow one didn't feel it would have been very wrong – would have only been addressing Christ sub specie Apollinis. *We witnessed a beautiful Christian village ceremony in Rhodes and hardly felt a discrepancy. Greek priests impress one very favourably at sight – much more so than most Protestant or RC clergy. And the peasants* refuse *tips.*

Letters

May

MAY IS THE MONTH OF HIGH spring, with plants and trees full of vitality, colour and flowers. Sunny without being too hot, it allows for work in the garden, long country walks and a general enjoyment of being outdoors after the enclosure of winter.

As spring brings forth the plants that began growing in the darker months, so spring also brought forth the publication of several of Jack Lewis's books – *The Pilgrim's Regress* in 1933, *Miracles* in 1947, and the first 'Screwtape Letter' in a church magazine called *The Guardian* in 1941 – all books which have over the years influenced thousands of lives.

In May 1862 Flora, Jack's beloved mother, was born, and though he wrote comparatively little about her, it was clear that she was the parent who brought love, fun and tranquillity into his childhood. Although Albert, his father, played a more prominent part in Jack's life, and Jack both loved and admired him, at the same time he recognized Albert's eccentricities and his generally gloomy outlook on life.

Jack Lewis's parents were very different in character. It was Flora, his mother, who gave a sense of peace and stability to the household and when she died, Jack, aged nine, felt that his world had fallen apart. She came from a long line of Anglican clergy, and was one of the first women to gain a university degree.

My mother had been a promising mathematician in her youth and a B.A. of Queen's College, Belfast, and before her death was able to start me both in French and Latin. She was a voracious reader of good novels, and I think the Merediths and Tolstoys which I have inherited were bought for her.

Albert Lewis, Jack's father, was a police court solicitor, with a generally gloomy outlook on life quite different from that of his wife. Albert, of course, had sole responsibility for the two boys after Flora's death, and in his own way did his utmost to give them a respectable home life, a proper education and a good start in life.

He was fond of oratory and had himself spoken on political platforms in England as a young man; if he had had independent means he would certainly have aimed at a political career... He had many of the gifts once needed by a Parliamentarian – a fine presence, a resonant voice, great quickness of mind, eloquence, and memory ... He greatly enjoyed nearly all humorous authors, from Dickens to W.W. Jacobs, and was himself, almost without rival, the best raconteur *I have ever heard; the best, that is, of his own type, the type that acts all the characters in turn with a free use of grimace, gesture, and pantomime. He was never happier than when closeted for an hour or so with one or two of my uncles exchanging 'wheezes' (as anecdotes were oddly called in our family) ...*

My father, whom I implicitly believed, represented adult life as one of incessant drudgery under the continual threat of financial ruin. In this he did not mean to deceive us. Such was his temperament that when he exclaimed, as he frequently did, 'There'll soon be nothing for it but the workhouse,' he momentarily believed, or at least felt, what he said. I took it all literally and had the gloomiest anticipation of adult life.

Surprised by Joy

One of the great joys in Jack Lewis's life in Oxford was to be a member of 'The Inklings', a group of friends who met on Thursday evenings in his rooms at Magdalen College to talk and to read aloud whatever each of them was then writing, and on Tuesday mornings in the back room of a pub called 'The Eagle and Child' (nicknamed 'The Bird and Baby'). One of their members was Charles Williams, and when he died in 1945 Jack wrote to a fellow Inkling, Owen Barfield.

Thanks for writing. It has been a very odd *experience. This, the first really severe loss I have suffered, has (a) Given a corroboration to my belief in immortality such as I never dreamed of. It is almost tangible now. (b) Swept away all my old feelings of mere horror and disgust at funerals, coffins, graves, etc. If need had been I think I could have handled* that *corpse with hardly any unpleasant sensations. (c) Greatly reduced my feelings about ghosts. I think (but who knows?) that I should be, though afraid, more pleased than afraid, if his turned up. In fact, all very curious. Great pain but no mere depression.*

Dyson said to me yesterday that he thought what was true of Christ was, in its lower degree, true of all Christians – i.e. they go away to return in a closer form and it is expedient for us that they should go away in order that they may do so. How foolish it is to imagine one can imaginatively foresee what any event will be like! 'Local unique sting' all right of course for I love him (I cannot say more) as much as you: and yet – a sort of brightness and tingling …

To put it in a nutshell – what the idea of death has done for him is nothing to what he has done to the idea of death. Hit it for six. Yet it used to rank as a fast bowler!

Letters

The first book that Jack Lewis wrote after becoming a Christian was *The Pilgrim's Regress*, an attempt to explain what he meant by 'Joy'. It was also his first prose work. After a few false starts, Lewis wrote the whole book during a fortnight's holiday in Ireland in 1932, and it was published in May 1933. In this extract John, the central character, rebels against the local Steward and sets off to find his dream.

I dreamed of a boy who was born in the land of Puritania and his name was John. And I dreamed that when John was able to walk he ran out of his parents' garden on a fine morning on to the road. And on the other side of the road there was a deep wood, but not thick, full of primroses and soft green moss. When John set eyes on this he thought he had never seen anything so beautiful: and he ran across the road and into the wood, and was just about to go down on his hands and knees and to pull up the primroses by handfuls, when his mother came running out of the garden gate, and she also ran across the road, and caught John up, and smacked him soundly and told him he must never go into the wood again. And John cried, but he asked no questions, for he was not yet at the age for asking questions. Then a year went past. And then, another fine morning, John had a little sling and he went out into the garden and he saw a bird sitting on a branch. And John got his sling ready and was going to have a shot at the bird, when the cook came running out of the garden and caught John up and smacked him soundly and told him he must never kill any of the birds in the garden.

 'Why?' said John.

 'Because the Steward would be very angry,' said cook.

 'Who is the Steward?' said John.

 'He is the man who makes rules for all the country round here,' said cook.

 'Why?' said John.

 'Because the Landlord set him to do it.'

 'Who is the Landlord?' said John.

 'He owns all the country,' said the cook.

'Why?' said John. And when he asked this, the cook went and told his mother.

And his mother sat down and talked to John about the Landlord all afternoon: but John took none of it in, for he was not yet at the age for taking it in. Then a year went past, and one dark, cold, wet morning John was made to put on new clothes … and his father and mother took him along the road … to see the Steward …

The Steward then took down from a peg a big card with small print all over it, and said, 'Here is a list of all the things the Landlord says you must not do. You'd better look at it.' So John took the card: but half the rules seemed to forbid things he had never heard of, and the other half forbade things he was doing every day and could not imagine not doing …

'Please, sir, supposing I did break one, one little one, just by accident, you know. Could nothing stop the snakes and lobsters?'

'Ah!' said the Steward; and then he sat down and talked for a long time, but John could not understand a single syllable …

Now the days and the weeks went on again, and I dreamed that John had little peace either by day or night for thinking of the rules and the black hole full of snakes … And now I dreamed that John went out one morning and tried to play in the road and to forget his troubles; but the rules kept coming back into his head … However, he went on always a few yards further till suddenly he looked up and … it seemed to him that a mist which hung at the end of the wood had parted for a moment, and through the rift he had seen a calm sea, and in the sea an island … and presently he went home, with a sad excitement about him, repeating to himself a thousand times, 'I know now what I want' … I dreamed that I saw John growing tall and lank till he ceased to be a child and became a boy. The chief pleasure of his life was … seeing the beautiful Island …

One night he was trudging home when he began to weep … A coach had gone past him … and he thought he heard a voice say, 'Come' … That night he waited till his parents were asleep, and … he stole out of the back door and set his face to the West to seek for the Island.

The Pilgrim's Regress

It was in the summer of 1940 that Lewis conceived the idea of letters between a senior devil and a junior one, and the first letter was published in a church magazine called *The Guardian* in May 1941. In what seems a light-hearted way the senior devil, Screwtape, writing to his nephew, Wormwood, subtly presents the art of moral seduction.

My dear Wormwood,

I note what you say about guiding your patient's reading and taking care that he sees a good deal of his materialist friend. But are you not being a trifle naif? It sounds as if you supposed that argument *was the way to keep him out of the Enemy's clutches. That might have been so if he had lived a few centuries earlier. At that time the humans still knew pretty well when a thing was proved and when it was not; and if it was proved they really believed it. They still connected thinking with doing, and were prepared to alter their way of life as the result of a chain of reasoning. But what with the weekly press and other such weapons we have largely altered that. Your man has been accustomed, ever since he was a boy, to have a dozen incompatible philosophies dancing about together inside his head. He doesn't think of doctrines as primarily 'true' or 'false', but as 'academic' or 'practical', 'outworn' or 'contemporary', 'conventional' or 'ruthless'. Jargon, not argument, is your best ally in keeping him from the Church. Don't waste time trying to make him think that materialism is* true! *Make him think it is strong, or stark, or courageous – that it is the philosophy of the future. That's the sort of thing he cares about.*

The trouble about argument is that it moves the whole struggle on to the Enemy's own ground. He can argue too; whereas in really practical propaganda of the kind I am suggesting He has been shown for centuries to be greatly the inferior of Our Father Below. By the very act of arguing, you awake the patient's reason; and once it is awake, who can foresee the result? Even if a particular train of thought can be twisted so as to end in our favour, you will find that you have been strengthening in your patient the fatal habit of attending to universal issues and withdrawing his attention from the stream of immediate sense experiences. Your business is to fix his attention on the stream. Teach him to call it 'real life' and don't let him ask what he means by 'real'.

Remember, he is not, like you, a pure spirit. Never having been a human (Oh that abominable advantage of the Enemy's!) you don't realize how enslaved they are to the pressure of the ordinary. I once had a patient, a sound atheist, who used to read in the British Museum. One day, as he sat reading, I saw a train of thought in his mind beginning to go the wrong way. The Enemy, of course, was at his elbow in a moment. Before I knew where I was I saw my twenty years' work beginning to totter. If I had lost my head and begun to attempt a defence by argument I should have been undone. But I was not such a fool. I struck instantly at the part of the man which I had best under my control and suggested that it was just about time he had some lunch. The Enemy presumably made the counter-suggestion (you know how one can never quite overhear what He says to them?) that this was more important than lunch. At least I think that must have been His line for when I said 'Quite. In fact much too important to tackle at the end of a morning,' the patient brightened up considerably; and by the time I had added 'Much better come back after lunch and go into it with a fresh mind,' he was already half-way to the door. Once he was in the street the battle was won. I showed him a newsboy shouting the midday paper, and a No. 73 bus going past, and before he reached the bottom of the steps I had got into him an unalterable conviction that, whatever odd ideas might come into a man's head when he was shut up alone with his books, a healthy dose of 'real life' (by which he meant the bus and the newsboy) was enough to show him that all 'that sort of thing' just couldn't be true. He knew he'd had a narrow escape ... He is now safe in Our Father's house.

Your affectionate uncle,
Screwtape

The Screwtape Letters

In the early centuries of the Christian Church most people believed in miracles, but with modern science viewing the world as entirely subject to the laws of Nature, by the time of Lewis's conversion even most theologians no longer believed in them. Encouraged by the writer Dorothy L. Sayers, Lewis began to expand his earlier thinking on the subject, and in May 1947 *Miracles* was published.

In all my life I have met only one person who claims to have seen a ghost. And the interesting thing about the story is that that person disbelieved in the immortal soul before she saw the ghost and still disbelieves after seeing it … Seeing is not believing.

For this reason, the question whether miracles occur can never be answered simply by experience. Every event which might claim to be a miracle is, in the last resort, something presented to our senses, something seen, heard, touched, smelled, or tasted. And our senses are not infallible. If anything extraordinary seems to have happened, we can always say that we have been the victims of an illusion …

If immediate experience cannot prove or disprove the miraculous, still less can history do so. Many people think one can decide whether a miracle occurred in the past by examining the evidence 'according to the ordinary rules of historical enquiry'. But the ordinary rules cannot be worked until we have decided whether miracles are possible, and if so, how probable they are. For if they are impossible, then no amount of historical evidence will convince us. If they are possible but immensely improbable, then only mathematically demonstrative evidence will convince us: and since history never provides that degree of evidence for any event, history can never convince us that a miracle occurred. If, on the other hand, miracles are not intrinsically improbable, then the existing evidence will be sufficient to convince us that quite a number of miracles have occurred. The result of our historical enquiries thus depends on the philosophical views which we have been holding before we even began to look at the evidence …

I use the word miracle to mean an interference with Nature by supernatural power … Unless there exists, in addition to Nature, something else which we may call the supernatural, there can be no miracles. Some people believe that nothing exists except Nature; I call these people Naturalists. *Others think that, besides Nature, there exists something else: I call them*

Supernaturalists ... *The Naturalist believes that a great process, or 'becoming', exists 'on its own' in space and time, and that nothing else exists ... The Supernaturalist believes that one Thing exists on its own and has produced the framework of space and time and the procession of systematically connected events which fill them ... It by no means follows from Supernaturalism that miracles of any sort do in fact occur. God (the primary thing) may never in fact interfere with the natural system He has created ... If Naturalism is true, then we do know in advance that miracles are impossible: nothing can come into Nature from the outside because there is nothing outside to come in, Nature being everything ... Our first choice, therefore, must be between Naturalism and Supernaturalism ...*

If ... you now turn to study the historical evidence for yourself, begin with the New Testament and not with the books about it ...

You are probably quite right in thinking that you will never see a miracle done ... God does not shake miracles into Nature at random as if from a pepper-caster. They come on great occasions: they are found at the great ganglions of history – not of political or social history, but of that spiritual history which cannot be fully known by men ... Unless you live near a railway, you will not see trains go past your windows. How likely is it that you or I will be present when a peace treaty is signed, when a great scientific discovery is made, when a dictator commits suicide? That we should see a miracle is even less likely.

Miracles

June

JUNE IS THE MONTH WHICH TYPIFIES summer in England – the weather is usually good, the roses are coming into their best, and the countryside still has something of the vibrant green of young leaves. Keen walkers such as Jack Lewis are out enjoying the views, the whole burgeoning of Nature, and the very exercise of walking itself, sometimes with a friend, sometimes alone.

Jack's brother Warren (Warnie), his best friend and perhaps the greatest single influence on his young life, was born on 16 June 1895. He seems to have been the ideal elder brother, and the two boys, bereft of their mother, formed a strong bond that was to last until Jack's death in 1963.

In June 1917 Jack joined the army, and there met Paddy Moore, shortly to be killed in action in France. Lewis and Moore promised to care for the other's parent if either was killed in battle, a promise that Lewis kept, at great cost to himself, until Mrs Moore's death in 1951.

After the Lewis family had moved into the 'New House' and Warnie had been sent off to school in England, Jack was taught at home by his mother and by a governess. Described as a 'chatterbox', and with plenty of people in the house to talk to, Jack still had a lot of time to himself, so he made his own 'study' in one of the attics and set about writing a history of 'Animal-Land'.

Solitude was nearly always at my command, somewhere in the garden or somewhere in the house. I had now learned both to read and write; I had a dozen things to do.

What drove me to write was the extreme manual clumsiness from which I have always suffered. I attribute it to a physical defect which my brother and I inherit from our father: we have only one joint in the thumb … Whatever the cause, nature laid on me from birth an utter incapacity to make anything. With pencil and pen I was handy enough, and I can still tie as good a bow as ever lay on man's collar, but with a tool or a bat or a gun, a sleeve-link or a corkscrew, I have always been unteachable. It was this that forced me to write. I longed to make things, ships, houses, engines. Many sheets of cardboard and pairs of scissors I spoiled, only to turn from my hopeless failures in tears. As a last resort, as a pis aller, I was driven to write stories instead, little dreaming to what a world of happiness I was being admitted. You can do more with a castle in a story than with the best cardboard castle that ever stood on a nursery table.

I soon staked out a claim to one of the attics and made it 'my study'. Pictures, of my own making or cut from brightly coloured Christmas numbers of magazines, were nailed on the walls. There I kept my pen and inkpot and writing books and paintbox … Here my first stories were written, and illustrated, with enormous satisfaction. They were an attempt to combine my two chief literary pleasures – 'dressed animals' and 'knights-in-armour'. As a result, I wrote about chivalrous mice and rabbits who rode out in complete mail to kill not giants but cats. But already the mood of the systematizer was strong in me; the mood which led Trollope so endlessly to elaborate his Barsetshire. The Animal-Land which came into action in the holidays when my brother was home was a modern Animal-Land: it had to have trains and steamships if it was to be a country shared with him. It followed, of course, that the medieval Animal-Land about which I wrote my stories must be the same country at an earlier period; and of course the two periods must be properly connected. This led me from romancing to historiography: I set about writing a full history of Animal-Land. Though more than one version of this instructive work is extant, I never succeeded in bringing it down to modern times; centuries take a deal of filling when all the events have to come out of the historian's head. But there is one touch in the History *that I still recall with some pride. The chivalric adventures which filled my stories were in it alluded to very lightly, and the reader was warned that they might be 'only legends'. Somehow – but heaven knows how – I realized even then that a historian should adopt a critical attitude towards epic material. From history it was only a step to geography. There was soon a map of Animal-Land – several maps, all tolerably consistent. Then Animal-Land had to be geographically related to my brother's India, and India consequently lifted out of its place in the real world. We made it an island, with its north coast running along the track of the Himalayas; between it and Animal-Land my brother rapidly invented the principal steamship routes. Soon there was a whole world and a map of that world which used every colour in my paintbox. And those parts of that world which we regarded as our own – Animal-Land and India – were increasingly peopled with consistent characters.*

Surprised by Joy

After his unhappy stays at two schools in England, and before going to study with W.T. Kirkpatrick, Jack Lewis attended Campbell College, Belfast, for three months in 1910. Though it was only a mile from his home, Jack went there as a boarder, but with the proviso that he could go home every Sunday. At the College he was introduced to the writings of Matthew Arnold.

Much the most important thing that happened to me at Campbell was that I there read Sohrah and Rustum *in form under an excellent master whom we called Octie. I loved the poem at first sight and have loved it ever since. As the wet fog, in the first line, rose out of the Oxus stream, so out of the whole poem there rose and wrapped me round an exquisite, silvery coolness, a delightful quality of distance and calm, a grave melancholy. I hardly appreciated then, as I have since learned to do, the central tragedy; what enchanted me was the artist in Pekin with his ivory forehead and pale hands, the cypress in the queen's garden, the backward glance at Rustum's youth, the pedlars from Khabul, the hushed Chorasmian waste. Arnold gave me at once (and the best of Arnold gives me still) a sense not indeed of passionless vision, but of a passionate, silent gazing at things a long way off. And here observe how literature actually works. Parrot critics say that* Sohrah *is a poem for classicists, to be enjoyed only by those who recognize the Homeric echoes. But I, in Octie's form room (and on Octie peace be) knew nothing of Homer. For me the relation between Arnold and Homer worked the other way; when I came years later to read the* Iliad *I liked it partly because it was for me reminiscent of* Sohrah. *Plainly, it does not matter at what point you first break into the system of European poetry. Only keep your ears open and your mouth shut and everything will lead you to everything else in the end –* ogni parte ad ogni parte splende.

Surprised by Joy

Early in 1918, having caught 'trench fever' in wartime France, Jack Lewis was sent to a hospital in Le Treport for three weeks, a piece of good luck for any soldier, away from the fighting and the mud. In the hospital (a converted hotel), Jack was able to recuperate, and it was there that he first read some essays by G.K. Chesterton, a devout Christian, at a time when Jack himself was still resisting Christianity.

I ... read a volume of Chesterton's essays. I had never heard of him and had no idea of what he stood for; nor can I quite understand why he made such an immediate conquest of me. It might have been expected that my pessimism, my atheism, and my hatred of sentiment would have made him to me the least congenial of all authors. It would almost seem that Providence, or some 'second cause' of a very obscure kind, quite overrules our previous tastes when It decides to bring two minds together. Liking an author may be as involuntary and improbable as falling in love. I was by now a sufficiently experienced reader to distinguish liking from agreement. I did not need to accept what Chesterton said in order to enjoy it. His humour was of the kind which I like best – not 'jokes' imbedded in the page like currants in a cake, still less (what I cannot endure), a general tone of flippancy and jocularity, but the humour which is not in any way separable from the argument but is rather (as Aristotle would say) the 'bloom' on dialectic itself. The sword glitters not because the swordsman set out to make it glitter but because he is fighting for his life and therefore moving it very quickly. For the critics who think Chesterton frivolous or 'paradoxical' I have to work hard to feel even pity; sympathy is out of the question. Moreover, strange as it may seem, I liked him for his goodness. I can attribute this taste to myself freely (even at that age) because it was a liking for goodness which had nothing to do with any attempt to be good myself. I have never felt the dislike of goodness which seems to be quite common in better men than me ... It was a matter of taste: I felt the 'charm' of goodness as a man feels the charm of a woman he has no intention of marrying. It is, indeed, at that distance that its 'charm' is most apparent.

Surprised by Joy

Lewis preached many fine sermons, but 'The Weight of Glory' (first preached in St Mary's Church, Oxford, on 8 June 1941) is one of the most impressive. Necessary for an understanding of his idea of 'Joy', it sets out to make Heaven desirable to all Christians – none of whom are *ordinary* people, for every Christian neighbour is holy because Christ is hidden in him or her.

I turn next to the idea of glory. There is no getting away from the fact that this idea is very prominent in the New Testament and in early Christian writings. Salvation is constantly associated with palms, crowns, white robes, thrones, and splendour like the sun and stars. All this makes no immediate appeal to me at all, and in that respect I fancy I am a typical modern …

When I began to look into this matter I was shocked to find such different Christians as Milton, Johnson and Thomas Aquinas taking heavenly glory quite frankly in the sense of fame or good report. But not fame conferred by our fellow creatures – fame with God, approval or (I might say) 'appreciation' by God. And then, when I had thought it over, I saw that this view was scriptural: nothing can eliminate from the parable the divine accolade, 'Well done, thou good and faithful servant' … No one can enter heaven except as a child; and nothing is so obvious in a child – not in a conceited child, but in a good child – as its great undisguised pleasure in being praised …

Perhaps it seems rather crude to describe glory as the fact of being 'noticed' by God. But this is almost the language of the New Testament. St Paul promises to those who love God not, as we should expect, that they will know Him, but that they will be known by Him (1 Corinthians 8:3). It is a strange promise. Does not God know all things at all times? …

The cross comes before the crown and tomorrow is a Monday morning. A cleft has opened in the pitiless walls of the world, and we are invited to follow our great Captain outside. The following Him is, of course, the essential point … It may be possible for each to think too much of his own potential glory hereafter; it is hardly possible for him to think too often or too deeply about that of his neighbour. The load, or weight, or burden of my neighbour's glory should be laid daily on my back, a load so heavy that only humility can carry it, and the backs of the proud will be broken. It is a serious thing to live in a society of possible gods and goddesses, to remember that the dullest and most uninteresting person you can talk to may one day be a creature which, if you saw it now, you would be strongly tempted to worship, or else a horror and a corruption such as you now meet, if at all, only in a nightmare. All day long we are, in some degree, helping each other to one or other of these destinations. It is in the light of these overwhelming possibilities, it is with the awe and the circumspection proper to them, that we should conduct all our dealings with one another, all friendships, all loves, all play, all politics. There are no ordinary people. You have never talked to a mere mortal. Nations, cultures, arts, civilizations – these are mortal, and their life is to ours as the life of a gnat. But it is immortals whom we joke with, work with, marry, snub, and exploit – immortal horrors or everlasting splendours. This does not mean that we are to be perpetually solemn. We must play. But our merriment must be of that kind (and it is, in fact, the merriest kind) which exists between people who have, from the outset, taken each other seriously – no flippancy, no superiority, no presumption. And our charity must be a real and costly love, with deep feeling for the sins in spite of which we love the sinner – no mere tolerance, or indulgence which parodies love as flippancy parodies merriment. Next to the Blessed Sacrament itself, your neighbour is the holiest object presented to your senses. If he is your Christian neighbour he is holy in almost the same way, for in him the Christ vere latitat *– the glorifier and the glorified, Glory Himself – is truly hidden.*

'*The Weight of Glory*' *in* Screwtape Proposes a Toast and other pieces

In the 6 June 1962 issue of *The Christian Century*, in response to the question, 'What books did most to shape your vocational attitude and your philosophy of life?' Lewis gave the following list.

Phantastes *by George MacDonald*
The Everlasting Man *by G.K. Chesterton*
The Aeneid *by Virgil*
The Temple *by George Herbert*
The Prelude *by William Wordsworth*
The Idea of the Holy *by Rudolf Otto*
The Consolation of Philosophy *by Boethius*
Life of Samuel Johnson *by James Boswell*
Descent into Hell *by Charles Williams*
Theism and Humanism *by Arthur James Balfour*

The Christian Century

Warren (Warnie) Lewis, born in Belfast in 1895, elder brother and lifelong friend of Jack, was a professional soldier for much of his life. He retired from the army to live with Jack in Oxford, where he acted as his secretary and handled his correspondence. An author and historian in his own right, specializing in seventeenth- and eighteenth-century France, Warnie was also a member of The Inklings, as well as editor of the eleven volumes of the Lewis family papers.

Once in those very early days my brother brought into the nursery the lid of a biscuit tin which he had covered with moss and garnished with twigs and flowers so as to make it a toy garden or a toy forest. That was the first beauty I ever knew. What the real garden had failed to do, the toy garden did. It made me aware of nature – not, indeed, as a storehouse of forms and colours but as something cool, dewy, fresh, exuberant …

My brother, as you know, was serving in France. From 1914 to 1916 … he becomes a figure that at rare intervals appears unpredicted on leave, in all the glory of a young officer, with what then seemed unlimited wealth at his command, and whisks me off to Ireland. Luxuries hitherto unknown to me, such as first class railway carriages and sleeping cars, glorify these journeys. You will understand that I had been crossing the Irish Sea six times a year since I was nine. My brother's leaves now often added journeys extraordinary … These leaves were of course a great delight … There was a tacit determination on both sides to revive, for the short time allowed us, the classic period of our boyhood. As my brother was to be in the RASC [Royal Army Service Corps], which in those days was reckoned a safe place to be, we did not feel that degree of anxiety about him which most families were suffering at this time …

Surprised by Joy

We have had so many alarms about you that I shall hardly believe it till I see you with my own eyes … you had been captured by bandits – were in jail – had gone mad – had married – had married a Chinese woman … It all seems too good to be true. I can hardly believe that when you take your shoes off a week or so hence [December 1932], please God, you will be able to say, 'This will do me – for life.'

Letters

July

BY THE TIME JULY COMES, SUMMER is well settled in Britain, the greens of leaves and grass are darker, the colours of flowers are brighter and more varied, and sitting outside in the cool of the evening is a lovely end to the day.

For Jack Lewis July was a month of mixed blessings. On the academic side, he took a First in English Language and Literature in 1923, conceived the idea for *The Screwtape Letters* in 1940, and his *Broadcast Talks* were published in 1942. But on the health front, things were gloomy: his father was found to have cancer in 1929; Joy, his wife, died in 1960; and in 1963 Jack himself went into hospital after a heart attack.

Perhaps the brightest July memory that Jack had was of the ten happy days he spent in Ireland with Joy in 1958, together with his long-time friend Arthur Greeves.

Albert Lewis, bereft of his wife, did not have an easy relationship with his sons. Jack in particular, who was at home more than Warnie, found his father difficult, although he loved and respected him and accepted his eccentricities.

Our father was out of the house from nine in the morning till six at night. From the very first we built up for ourselves a life that excluded him. He on his part demanded a confidence even more boundless, perhaps, than a father usually, or wisely demands. One instance of this, early in my life, has far-reaching effects. Once when I was at Oldie's and had just begun to try to live as a Christian I wrote out a set of rules for myself and put them in my pocket. On the first day of the holidays, noticing that my pockets bulged with all sorts of paper and that my coat was being pulled out of all shape, he plucked out the whole pile of rubbish and began to go through it. Boylike, I would have died rather than let him see my list of good resolutions. I managed to keep them out of his reach and get them into the fire. I do not see that either of us was to blame; but never from that moment until the hour of his death did I enter his house without first going through my own pockets and removing anything that I wished to keep private. A habit of concealment was thus bred before I had anything guilty to conceal …

You will have grasped that my father was no fool. He even had a streak of genius in him. At the same time he had – when seated in his own armchair after a heavy midday dinner on an August afternoon with all the windows shut – more power of confusing an issue or taking up a fact wrongly than any man I have ever known. As a result it was impossible to drive into his head any of the realities of our school life, after which (nevertheless) he repeatedly enquired. The first and simplest barrier to communication was that, having earnestly asked, he did not 'stay for an answer', or forgot it the moment it was uttered. Some facts must have been asked for and told him on a moderate computation, once a week and were received by him each time as perfect novelties. But this was the simplest barrier. Far more often he retained something, but something very unlike what you had said. His mind so bubbled over with humour, sentiment, and indignation that, long before he had understood or even listened to your words, some accidental hint had set his imagination to work, he had produced his own version of the facts, and believed he was getting it from you. As he invariably got proper names wrong (no name seemed less probable than another) his textus receptus *was often almost unrecognizable. Tell him that a boy called Churchwood had caught a fieldmouse and kept it as a pet, and a year, or even ten years later, he would ask you, 'Did you ever hear what became of poor Chickweed who was so afraid of rats?' For his own version, once adopted, was indelible, and attempts to correct it only produced an incredulous 'Hm! Well, that's not the story you* used *to tell'… Hence he who in real life was the most honourable and impulsive of men, and the easiest victim that any knave or impostor could hope to meet, became a positive Machiavel when he knitted his brows and applied to the behaviour of people he had never seen the spectral and labyrinthine operation which he called 'reading between the lines'. Once embarked upon that, he might make his landfall anywhere in the wide world: and always with unshakeable conviction …*

I would not commit the sin of Ham. Nor would I, as historian, reduce a complex character to a false simplicity. The man who, in his armchair, sometimes appeared not so much incapable of understanding anything as determined to misunderstand everything, was formidable in the police court and, I presume, efficient in his office.

Surprised by Joy

Although Jack and his father had a difficult relationship, there was real affection on both sides, and when in July 1929 Albert was diagnosed as having cancer, Jack was deeply distressed. As soon as he could leave his university work, he went home and spent the next weeks nursing his father. Here is Jack's reply to Albert's letter telling of his illness.

My dear, dear Papy,

I am very glad you have written. I had heard the news and was anxious to write, but hardly knew how to do so. I will, of course, come home at the first moment … there is surer ground – at least for you – in the wonderful spirit, as shown in your letter, with which you are taking it. I wish I could convey to you one tithe of the respect and affection which I felt in reading it. For the rest, what can I say to you that is not already understood? … It has been a bit of a strain this last week to keep my mind on examination papers for nine hours a day, and I am especially glad that you have written. Whatever the next few days bring forth I hope you will make no decision about your treatment without letting me know … With all my love and my best wishes – I wish there was anything more useful I could offer – your loving son …

Jack nursed his father from 13 August, and wrote to Warnie after Albert's death.

By this time you will have had my cable and the two letters … The operation, in spite of what they prophesied, discovered cancer. They said he might live a few years. I remained at home, visiting him in the Nursing Home, for ten days. There were ups and downs … but nothing really dreadful. Quite often he was himself and telling wheezes, though of course he was often wandering from the dopes. By this time I had been at home since 11th August and my work for next term was getting really desperate, and as Joey [cousin and blood specialist] said, I might easily wait several weeks more and still be in the same position – i.e. not really making the progress he should, but not likely to take a turn for the worse. I therefore crossed to Oxford on Saturday 22nd September. On Tuesday 24th I got a wire saying that he was worse, caught the train an hour later, and arrived to find that he had died on Tuesday afternoon.

Letters

One evening in July 1940, some ten months after the start of the Second World War, listening to Hitler on the radio, Lewis realized how easy it is to be persuaded to believe something if the argument is presented firmly enough. The next morning, in church, the idea came to him of letters from a senior devil to a junior, and *The Screwtape Letters* were born.

I have been to church for the first time for many weeks owing to the illness, and considered myself invalid enough to make a midday communion … Before the service was over – one could wish these things came more seasonably – I was struck by an idea for a book which I think might be both useful and entertaining. It would be called As one Devil to Another *and would consist of letters from an elderly retired devil to a young devil who has just started work on his first 'patient'. The idea would be to give all the psychology of temptation from the* other *point of view, e.g. 'About undermining his faith in prayer, I don't think you need have any difficulty with his intellect, provided you never say the wrong thing at the wrong moment. After all, the Enemy will either answer his prayers or not. If He does* not, *then that's simple – it shows prayers are no good. If He does – I've always found that, oddly enough, this can be just as easily utilized. It needs only a word from you to make him believe that the very fact of feeling more patient after he's prayed for patience will be taken as a proof that prayer is a kind of self-hypnosis. Or if it is answered by some external event, then since that event will have causes which you can point to, he can be persuaded that it would have happened anyway. You see the idea? Prayer can always be discredited either because it works or because it doesn't.' Or again: 'In attacking faith, I should be chary of argument. Arguments only provoke answers. What you want to work away at is the mere unreasoning* feeling *that "that sort of thing can't really be true"'…*

Letters

In July 1942 *Broadcast Talks*, which combined the first two series of radio talks given by Lewis – *Right and Wrong* and *What Christians Believe* – was published. Lewis was again overwhelmed with letters. 'I wrote 35 letters yesterday,' he told the BBC producer. The book was well received, one reviewer saying that Lewis was 'a master in the rare art of conveying profound truths in simple and compelling language'.

If you are a Christian you do not have to believe that all the other religions of the whole world are simply wrong all through. If you are an atheist you do have to believe that the main point in all the religions of the whole world is simply one huge mistake ... When I was an atheist I had to try to persuade myself that most of the human race have always been wrong about the question that mattered to them most; when I became a Christian I was able to take a more liberal view. But, of course, being a Christian does mean thinking that where Christianity differs from other religions, Christianity is right and they are wrong. As in arithmetic – there is only one right answer to a sum, and all other answers are wrong; but some of the wrong answers are much nearer being right than others.

The first big division of humanity is into the majority, who believe in some kind of God or gods, and the minority who do not. On this point, Christianity lines up with the majority – lines up with ancient Greeks and Romans, modern savages, Stoics, Platonists, Hindus, Muhammadans, etc., against the modern Western European materialist ...

People who all believe in God can be divided according to the sort of God they believe in. There are two very different ideas on this subject. One of them is the idea that He is beyond good and evil ... These people would say that the wiser you become the less you would want to call anything good or bad, and the more clearly you would see that everything is good in one way and bad in another, and that nothing could have been different ... The other and opposite idea is that God is quite definitely 'good' or 'righteous', a God who takes sides, who loves love and hates hatred, who wants us to behave in one way and not in another. The first of these views ... is called Pantheism ... The other view is held by Jews, Muhammadans and Christians ...

Pantheists usually believe that God, so to speak, animates the universe as you animate your body: that the universe almost is God, so that if it did not exist He would not exist either ... The Christian idea is quite different. They think God invented and made the universe – like a man making a picture or composing a tune ...

Christianity is a fighting religion. It thinks God made the world ... But it also thinks that a great many things have gone wrong with the world that God made and that God insists, and insists very loudly, on our putting them right again.

And, of course, that raises a very big question. If a good God made the world why has it gone wrong? And for many years I simply refused to listen to the Christian answers to this question, because I kept on feeling 'whatever you say, and however clever your arguments are, isn't it much simpler and easier to say that the world was not made by any intelligent power? Aren't all your arguments simply a complicated attempt to avoid the obvious? ...

My argument against God was that the universe seemed so cruel and unjust. But how had I got this idea of just and unjust? A man does not call a line crooked unless he has some idea of a straight line. What was I comparing this universe with when I called it unjust? ... I could have given up my idea of justice by saying it was nothing but a private idea of my own. But if I did that, then my argument against God collapsed too – for the argument depended on saying that the world was really unjust, not simply that it did not happen to please my fancies. Thus in the very act of trying to prove that God did not exist – in other words, that the whole of reality was senseless – I found I was forced to assume that one part of reality – namely my idea of justice – was full of sense. Consequently atheism turns out to be too simple. If the whole universe has no meaning, we should never have found out that it has no meaning: just as, if there were no light in the universe and therefore no creatures with eyes, we should never know it was dark. Dark would be a word without meaning.

'What Christians Believe' in Mere Christianity

Jack had spent over 50 years of his life as a bachelor, but in March 1957 he married Joy Davidman, an American divorcée with two growing sons. The following July, when Joy's cancer had been diagnosed as arrested, she and Jack spent two weeks on holiday in Ireland, with Jack's boyhood friend, Arthur Greeves. It was Joy's first trip there, and they treated it as a belated honeymoon, giving Jack an opportunity to introduce his wife to his Irish relations, who enjoyed meeting her. Back in Oxford, Jack wrote to a friend:

All goes amazing well with us. My wife walks up the wooded hill behind our house and shoots – or more strictly shoots at pigeons, picks peas and beans, and heaven knows what.

We had a holiday – you might call it a belated honeymoon – in Ireland and were lucky enough to get that perfect fortnight at the beginning of July. We visited Louth, Down, and Donegal, and returned drunk with blue mountains, yellow beaches, dark fuchsia, breaking waves, braying donkeys, peat smell, and the heather then just beginning to bloom.

We flew to Ireland, for, though both of us would prefer ship to plane, her bones, and even mine, could not risk a sudden lurch. It was the first flight either of us had ever experienced and we found it, after one initial moment of terror, enchanting. The cloud-scape seen from above is a new world of beauty – and then the rifts in the clouds through which one sees (like Tennyson's Tithonus) 'a glimpse of that dark world where I was born'. We had clear weather over the Irish Sea and the first Irish headland, brightly sunlit, stood out from the dark sea (it's very dark when you're looking directly down *on it) like a bit of enamel.*

As for the picture in The Observer, *even our most ribald friends don't pretend it has any resemblance to either of us. [The photo accompanied Jack's essay 'Willing Slaves of the Welfare State'.] As a spiritualist picture of the ectoplasms of a dyspeptic orang-utan and an immature Sorn it may have its merits, but not as a picture of us …*

Letters

Despite all the other challenges and all the academic successes of his life, Jack's marriage to Joy was to bring him the deepest happiness and fulfilment, and when she finally died of cancer after only three short years together, Jack's grief was intense. Two days later he wrote to a friend:

Alas, you will never send anything along 'for the three of us' again, for my dear Joy is dead. Until within ten days of the end we hoped, although noticing her increasing weakness, that she was going to hold her own, but it was not to be.

Last week she had been complaining of muscular pains in her shoulders, but by Monday 11th seemed much better, and on Tuesday, though keeping her bed, said she felt a great improvement: on that day she was in good spirits, did her crossword puzzle with me, and in the evening played a game of Scrabble. At quarter past six on Wednesday morning (13th July) my brother, who slept over her, was wakened by her screaming and ran down to her. I got the doctor, who fortunately was at home, and he arrived before seven and gave her a heavy shot. At half past one I took her into hospital in an ambulance. She was conscious for the short remainder of her life, and in very little pain thanks to drugs: and died peacefully in my company about 10.15 the same night …

You will understand that I have no heart to write more, but I hope that when next I send a letter it will be a less depressing one.

Three weeks later Lewis wrote again:

I believe in the resurrection … but the state of the dead till *the resurrection is unimaginable. Are they in the same* time *that we live in at all? And if not, is there any sense in asking where they are 'now'? …*

Perhaps being maddeningly busy is the best thing for me. Anyway I am. This is one of those things which makes the tragedies of real life so very *unlike those of the stage.*

Letters

August

WITH AUGUST, THE LAST FULL MONTH of summer, the countryside is heavy and lethargic in the heat. The harvest has left a few yellow fields, but mostly there is stubble on the brown earth and large mounds of hay. In Jack Lewis's day this was still kept in the form of traditional haystacks, and harvest was a time of hard work followed by social merriment. In an era before the tourist industry could offer breaks at all times of the year, August was the main holiday month. Lewis used it to gain refreshment, to catch up on his reading and to prepare for the coming academic year.

This was another month of mixed blessings for Jack. It saw the birth of his father in 1863, the marriage of his parents in 1894, but also the death of Flora, his mother, in 1908. After Joy's death in July 1960, August was also a time of intense grieving, but out of that sorrow came *A Grief Observed*, a book that was to bring comfort to so many other bereaved people over the years.

On 29 August 1894 Albert James Lewis married Florence Augusta (Flora) Hamilton at St Mark's Church, Dundela, Belfast. Albert had been educated at Lurgan College in County Armagh, where his headmaster was W.T. Kirkpatrick, who was later to have such an influence on Jack's education. Flora was the daughter of the Rector of St Mark's Church, whose grandfather had been a Bishop in the Church of Ireland.

Two very different strains had gone into our making. My father belonged to the first generation of his family that reached professional station. His grandfather had been a Welsh farmer; his father, a self-made man, had begun life as a workman, emigrated to Ireland, and ended as a partner in the firm of Macilwaine and Lewis, 'Boilermakers, Engineers, and Iron Ship Builders'.

My mother was a Hamilton with many generations of clergymen, lawyers, sailors, and the like behind her; on her mother's side, through the Warrens, the blood went back to a Norman knight whose bones lie at Battle Abbey.

The two families from which I spring were as different in temperament as in origin. My father's people were true Welshmen, sentimental, passionate, and rhetorical, easily moved both to anger and to tenderness; men who laughed and cried a great deal and who had not much of the talent for happiness. The Hamiltons were a cooler race. Their minds were critical and ironic and they had the talent for happiness in a high degree – went straight for it as experienced travellers go for the best seat in a train. From my earliest years I was aware of the vivid contrast between my mother's cheerful and tranquil affection, and the ups and downs of my father's emotional life, and this bred in me long before I was old enough to give it a name a certain distrust or dislike of emotion, as something uncomfortable and embarrassing and even dangerous.

Surprised by Joy

On one particular date, 23 August, two events of importance to Jack Lewis occurred. The first was the birth of his father, Albert, in 1863, which appeared to a young boy as merely a simple fact. The second was the death of his mother, Flora, in 1908, when Jack was nine, an event that was to alter the course of his life.

There came a night when I was ill and crying both with headache and toothache and distressed because my mother did not come to me. That was because she was ill too; and what was odd was that there were several doctors in her room, and voices, and comings and goings all over the house, and doors shutting and opening. It seemed to last for hours. And then my father, in tears, came into my room and began to try to convey to my terrified mind things it had never conceived before. It was in fact cancer and followed the usual course: an operation (they operated in the patient's house in those days), an apparent convalescence, a return of the disease, increasing pain, and death. My father never fully recovered from this loss ...

For us boys the real bereavement had happened before our mother died. We lost her gradually as she was gradually withdrawn from our life into the hands of nurses and delirium and morphia, and as our whole existence changed into something alien and menacing, as the house became full of strange smells and midnight noises and sinister whispered conversations ... The sight of adult misery and adult terror has an effect on children which is merely paralysing and alienating. Perhaps it was our fault. Perhaps if we had been better children we might have lightened our father's sufferings at this time. We certainly did not ... By a peculiar cruelty of fate, during those months the unfortunate man, had he but known it, was really losing his sons as well as his wife. We were coming, my brother and I, to rely more and more exclusively on each other for all that made life bearable ... Everything that had made the house a home had failed us; everything except one another. We drew daily closer together ... two frightened urchins huddled for warmth in a bleak world.

Surprised by Joy

After Joy's death, Jack spent part of August 1960 writing *A Grief Observed*. Originally intended simply for his own private help, Lewis decided to publish it anonymously and with a different publisher from his usual one. At Faber & Faber, the writer T.S. Eliot recognized Jack's writing and advised him to publish under an ordinary English pen name rather than the Latin one he had originally chosen. The book was published in 1961 under the name of N.W. Clerk. Even after all these years *A Grief Observed* continues to bring comfort to thousands of grieving people.

No one ever told me that grief felt so like fear. I am not afraid, but the sensation is like being afraid. The same fluttering in the stomach, the same restlessness, the yawning. I keep on swallowing.

At other times it feels like being mildly drunk, or concussed. There is a sort of invisible blanket between the world and me. I find it hard to take in what anyone says. Or perhaps, hard to want to take it in. It is so uninteresting. Yet I want the others to be about me. I dread the moments when the house is empty. If only they would talk to one another and not to me.

There are moments, most unexpectedly, when something inside me tries to assure me that I don't really mind so much, not so very much, after all. Love is not the whole of a man's life. I was happy before I ever met H. I've plenty of what are called 'resources'. People get over these things. Come, I shan't do so badly. One is ashamed to listen to this voice but it seems for a little to be making out a good case. Then comes a sudden jab of red-hot memory and all this 'commonsense' vanishes like an ant in the mouth of a furnace.

On the rebound one passes into tears and pathos. Maudlin tears. I almost prefer the moments of agony. These are at least clean and honest. But the bath of self-pity, the wallow, the loathsome sticky-sweet pleasure of indulging it – that disgusts me. And even while I'm doing it I know it leads me to misrepresent H. herself …

And no one ever told me about the laziness of grief. Except at my job – where the machine seems to run on much as usual – I loathe the slightest effort. Not only writing but even reading a letter is too much. Even shaving. What does it matter now whether my cheek is rough or smooth? …

Meanwhile, where is God? This is one of the most disquieting symptoms. When you are happy, so happy that you have no sense of needing Him, so happy that you are tempted to feel His claims upon you as an interruption, if you remember yourself and turn to Him with gratitude and praise, you will be – or so it feels – welcomed with open arms. But go to Him when your need is desperate, when all other help is vain, and what do you find? A door slammed in your face ... after that, silence ... Why is He so present a commander in our time of prosperity and so very absent a help in time of trouble? ...

I cannot talk to the children about her. The moment I try, there appears on their faces neither grief, nor love, nor fear, nor pity, but the most fatal of all non-conductors, embarrassment. They look as if I were committing an indecency. They are longing for me to stop. I felt just the same after my own mother's death when my father mentioned her. I can't blame them. It's the way boys are ...

It is hard to have patience with people who say 'There is no death' or 'Death doesn't matter.' There is death. And what-ever is matters ...

I have no photograph of her that's any good. I cannot even see her face distinctly in my imagination ... But her voice is still vivid. The remembered voice – that can turn me at any moment to a whimpering child ...

Once very near the end I said, 'If you can – if it is allowed – come to me when I too am on my death bed.' 'Allowed!' she said. 'Heaven would have a job to hold me; and as for Hell, I'd break it into bits!' She knew she was speaking a kind of mythological language, with even an element of comedy in it. There was a twinkle as well as a tear in her eye. But there was no myth and no joke about the will, deeper than any feeling, that flashed through her.

But I mustn't, because I have come to misunderstand a little less completely what a pure intelligence might be, lean over too far ... How wicked it would be, if we could, to call the dead back!

A Grief Observed

In August 1932, on a fortnight's holiday in Ireland with Arthur Greeves, Jack Lewis wrote *The Pilgrim's Regress*. In a Preface to the third edition (1943) he wrote:

On re-reading this book ten years after I wrote it, I find its chief faults to be those two which I myself least easily forgive in the books of other men: needless obscurity, and an uncharitable temper.

There were two causes, I now realize, for the obscurity. On the intellectual side my own progress had been from 'popular realism' to Philosophical Idealism; from Idealism to Pantheism; from Pantheism to Theism; and from Theism to Christianity. I still think this is a very natural road, but I now know that it is a road very rarely trodden. In the early thirties I did not know this. If I had had any notion of my own isolation, I should either have kept silent about my journey, or else endeavoured to describe it with more consideration for the reader's difficulties. As things were, I committed the same sort of blunder as one who should narrate his travels through the Gobi Desert on the assumption that this route was as familiar to the British public as the line from Euston to Crewe …

The second cause of obscurity was the (unintentionally) private meaning I then gave to the word 'Romanticism'. I would not now use this word to describe the experience which is central in this book. I would not, indeed, use it to describe anything, for I now believe it to be a word of such varying senses that it has become useless and should be banished from our vocabulary …

But what I meant by 'Romanticism' … was a particular recurrent experience which dominated my childhood and adolescence and which I hastily called 'Romantic' because inanimate nature and marvellous literature were among the things that evoked it …

The experience is one of intense longing. It is distinguished from other longings by two things. In the first place, though the sense of want is acute and even painful, yet the mere wanting is felt to be somehow a delight … This desire, even when there is no hope of possible satisfaction, continues to be prized, and even to be preferred to anything else in the world, by those who have once felt it … In the second place, there is a peculiar mystery about the object of this Desire. Inexperienced people (and inattention leaves some inexperienced all their lives) suppose, when they feel it, that they know what they are desiring … Every one of these supposed objects for the Desire is inadequate to it … If a man diligently followed this desire, pursuing the false objects until their falsity appeared and then resolutely abandoning them, he must come out at last into the clear knowledge that the human soul was made to enjoy some object that is never fully given … in our present mode of subjective and spatio-temporal experience. This Desire was, in the soul, as the Siege Perilous in Arthur's castle – the chair in which only one could sit. And if Nature makes nothing in vain, the One who can sit in this chair must exist …

After this explanation the reader will more easily understand (I do not ask him to condone) the bitterness of certain pages in this book. He will realize how the post-war period must have looked to one who had followed such a road as mine. The different intellectual movements of that time were hostile to one another; but the one thing that seemed to unite them all was their common enmity to 'immortal longings' … These people seemed to be condemning what they did not understand. When they called Romanticism 'nostalgia' I … felt that they had not even crossed the Pons Asinorum. *In the end I lost my temper …*

The book is concerned solely with Christianity as against unbelief … In this Preface the autobiographical element in John has had to be stressed because the source of the obscurities lay there. But you must not assume that everything in the book is autobiographical. I was attempting to generalize, not to tell people about my own life.

The Pilgrim's Regress

In 1941 Lewis gave the series of radio talks entitled *Right and Wrong*, which were to become Book I of *Mere Christianity*. He began by looking at the Law of Nature, the one law which mankind is free to disobey. Other laws, such as the law of gravity, cannot be disobeyed, but the Law of Nature – the human idea of decent behaviour – can be. Lewis argued that all civilizations, whatever their individual differences, have this idea in common.

Each man is at every moment subjected to several different sets of law but there is only one of these which he is free to disobey. As a body, he is subjected to gravitation and cannot disobey it; if you leave him unsupported in mid-air, he has no more choice about falling than a stone has. As an organism, he is subjected to various biological laws which he cannot disobey any more than an animal can. That is, he cannot disobey those laws which he shares with other things; but the law which is peculiar to his human nature, the law he does not share with animals or vegetables or inorganic things, is the one he can disobey if he chooses.

This law was called the Law of Nature because people thought that everyone knew it by nature and did not need to be taught it … Taking the race as a whole, they thought that the human idea of decent behaviour was obvious to everyone. And I believe they were right …

I hope you will not misunderstand what I am going to say. I am not preaching, and Heaven knows I do not pretend to be better than anyone else. I am only trying to call attention to a fact; the fact that this year, or this month, or, more likely, this very day, we have failed to practise ourselves the kind of behaviour we expect from other people. There may be all sorts of excuses for us. That time you were so unfair to the children was when you were very tired. That slightly shady business about the money – the one you have almost forgotten – came when you were very hard up. And what you promised to do for old So-and-So and have never done – well, you never would have promised if you had known how frightfully busy you were going to be. And as for your behaviour to your wife (or husband) or sister (or brother), if I knew how irritating they could be, I would not wonder at it – and who the dickens am I, anyway? I am just the same. That is to say, I do not succeed in keeping the Law of Nature very well, and the moment anyone tells me I am not keeping it, there starts up in my mind a string of excuses as long as your arm. The question at the moment is not whether they are good excuses. The point is that they are one more proof of how deeply, whether we like it or not, we believe in the Law of Nature. If we do not believe in decent behaviour, why should we be so anxious to make excuses for not having behaved decently? The truth is, we believe in decency so much – we feel the Rule or Law pressing on us so – that we cannot bear to face the fact that we are breaking it, and consequently we try to shift the responsibility. For you notice that it is only for our bad behaviour that we find all these explanations. It is only our bad temper that we put down to being tired or worried or hungry; we put our good temper down to ourselves.

These, then, are the two points I wanted to make. First, that human beings, all over the earth, have this curious idea that they ought to behave in a certain way, and cannot really get rid of it. Secondly, that they do not in fact have to behave in that way. They know the Law of Nature; they break it. These two facts are the foundation of all clear thinking about ourselves and the universe we live in.

'Right and Wrong' in Mere Christianity

September

SEPTEMBER IS A LOVELY MONTH IN Britain. It is late summer and, although the heat of August has gone, the sun is still there and many summer flowers are still blooming, but the evenings start earlier and there is a sense of coming change in the air.

With the forthcoming new academic year, it is a time of new beginnings, and for Jack Lewis there were several others: in 1914 he first met W.T. Kirkpatrick, the tutor who was to have such a profound effect on his whole life; in 1929 his father died; in 1939 the Second World War began; and in 1952 he first met Joy Davidman.

Most importantly of all, it was in September 1931 that Jack became certain that Jesus Christ is the Son of God, a realization that was to enrich his whole life and lead to so much writing for both adults and children.

In September 1914 Jack Lewis, then aged 15, arrived in Surrey to study under his father's old headmaster, William T. Kirkpatrick. Albert had told Jack about him, though with no great accuracy, but he was nevertheless an inspired choice, just what Jack needed. In the days when owning a car was rare, Kirkpatrick walked to the station to meet his new pupil. Here are Jack's recollections of their first meeting, at the local railway station.

He was over six feet tall, very shabbily dressed (like a gardener, I thought), lean as a rake, and immensely muscular. His wrinkled face seemed to consist entirely of muscles, so far as it was visible; for he wore moustache and side whiskers with a clean shaven chin … We shook hands … and … a few minutes later we were walking away from the station … I began to 'make conversation' in the deplorable manner which I had acquired at those evening parties and indeed found increasingly necessary to use with my father. I said I was surprised at the 'scenery' of Surrey; it was much 'wilder' than I had expected.

'Stop!' shouted Kirk with a suddenness that made me jump. 'What do you mean by wildness and what grounds had you for not expecting it?'

I replied I don't know what, still 'making conversation'. As answer after answer was torn to shreds it at last dawned upon me that he really wanted to know. He was not making conversation, not joking, not snubbing me; he wanted to know … If ever a man came near to being a purely logical entity, that man was Kirk … The idea that human beings should exercise their vocal organs for any purpose except that of communicating or discovering truth was to him preposterous. The most casual remark was taken as a summons to disputation. I soon came to know the differing values of his three openings … The most encouraging of all was 'I hear you'. This meant that your remark was significant and only required refutation; it had risen to the dignity of error. Refutation (when we got so far) always followed the same lines. Had I read this? Had I studied that? Had I any statistical evidence? Had I any evidence in my own experience? And so to the almost inevitable conclusion, 'Do you not see then that you had no right, etc.'

Surprised by Joy

Both Jack and Warnie had lost their Christian belief as young men, but in 1931 both found it again. Jack had resisted as long as he could, and he wrote movingly of it in his spiritual autobiography, *Surprised by Joy*, which was published in 1955.

You must picture me alone in that room at Magdalen, night after night, feeling, whenever my mind lifted for a second from my work, the steady, unrelenting approach of Him whom I so earnestly desired not to meet. That which I greatly feared had come upon me. In the Trinity Term of 1929 I gave in, and admitted that God was God, and knelt and prayed: perhaps, that night, the most dejected and reluctant convert in all England. I did not then see what is now the most shining and obvious thing; the Divine humility which will accept a convert even on such terms …

My conversion involved as yet no belief in a future life. I now number it among my greatest mercies that I was permitted for several months, perhaps for a year, to know God and to attempt obedience without even raising that question …

As I drew near the conclusion, I felt a resistance almost as strong as my previous resistance to theism. As strong, but shorter lived, for I understood it better … To recognize the ground for my evasion was of course to recognize both its shame and its futility. I know very well when, but hardly how, the final step was taken. I was driven to Whipsnade one sunny morning. When we set out I did not believe that Jesus Christ is the Son of God, and when we reached the zoo I did.

Surprised by Joy

On 29 September 1929 Albert Lewis died. Jack wrote:

I always before condemned as sentimentalists and hypocrites the people whose view of the dead was so different from the view they held of the same people living. Now one finds out that it is a natural process … I think mere pity for the poor old chap and for the life he had led really surmounted everything else … As time goes on the thing that emerges is that, whatever else he was, he was a terrific personality.

Letters

Before his conversion to theism, Lewis's writings were all to do with his main academic subject, English literature, in which he became a noted scholar, and to the end of his life it was with English that he earned his living. His lengthy poem *Dymer* had been published in 1926 under the pseudonym of 'Clive Hamilton', but in 1950 it was reissued, with emendations, and Lewis wrote in the Preface:

At its original appearance in 1926, Dymer, *like many better books, found some good reviews and almost no readers. The idea of disturbing its repose in the grave now comes from its publishers, not from me, but I have a reason for wishing to be present at the exhumation. Nearly a quarter of a century has gone since I wrote it, and in that time things have changed both within me and round me; my old poem might be misunderstood by those who now read it for the first time ... What I 'found', what simply 'came to me', was the story of a man who, on some mysterious bride, begets a monster: which monster, as soon as it has killed its father, becomes a god. This story arrived, complete, in my mind somewhere about my seventeenth year ... All I know is that there was a time when it was not there, and then presently a time when it was ...*

Preface to Dymer *in* Narrative Poems

Lewis was honoured to be asked to write Volume III of *The Oxford History of English Literature* (*OHEL*), entitled *English Literature in the 16th Century, excluding Drama*, published in 1954. He spent many long years on this work, which he often referred to as 'The *O HELL*'. In 1952 he wrote:

My year 'off' has been, as it was meant to be, so far a year of very hard work, but most congenial. The book really begins to look as if it might be finished in 1952 and I am, between ourselves, pleased with the manner of it – but afraid of hidden errors ... A mistake in a history of literature walks in silence till the day it turns irrevocable in a printed book and the book goes for review to the only man in England who would have known it for a mistake.

Letters

In 1956 *Till We Have Faces* was published, which Lewis described as the 'favourite of all my books', but 'my one big failure with both the critics and with the public'. Now generally regarded as a great book, Lewis dedicated it to Joy Davidman, who had helped him find the right idea. In a note for the American edition he wrote:

The story of Cupid and Psyche first occurs in one of the few surviving Latin novels, the Metamorphoses *(sometimes called* The Golden Ass*) of Lucius Apuleius Platonicus, who was born about* AD *125…*

The central alteration in my own version consists in making Psyche's palace invisible to normal, mortal eyes – if 'making' is not the wrong word for something which forced itself upon me, almost at my first reading of the story, as the way the thing must have been … I felt quite free to go behind Apuleius, whom I suppose to have been its transmitter, not its inventor …

This re-interpretation of an old story has lived in the author's mind, thickening and hardening with the years, ever since he was an undergraduate. That way, he could be said to have worked at it most of his life. Recently, what seemed to be the right form presented itself and themes suddenly interlocked: the straight tale of barbarism, the mind of an ugly woman, dark idolatry and pale enlightenment at war with each other and with vision, and the havoc which a vocation, or even a faith, works on human life.

Till We Have Faces

On 1 September 1939 Germany invaded Poland, and three days later Britain and Germany were at war. Foreseeing the likelihood that London would be bombed, the Government arranged for children to be sent away to safety, and thousands went. They were known as 'the evacuees', and Lewis and Mrs Moore (Minto) took in some of them. Lewis wrote to his brother Warnie:

Our schoolgirls have arrived and all seem to me – and what's more important, to Minto – to be very nice, unaffected creatures and all most flatteringly delighted with their new surroundings. They're fond of animals which is a good thing (for them as well as us) …

Life at The Kilns is going on at least as well as I expected. We had our first air raid warning at 7.45 the other morning when I expect you had yours too. Everyone got to the dug-out quite quickly and I must say they all behaved well, and though very hungry and thirsty before the all-clear went, we quite enjoyed the most perfect late summer morning I have ever seen. The main trouble of life at present is the blacking out which is done (as you may imagine) with a most complicated Arthur Rackham system of odd rags – quite effectively but at the cost of much labour …

Some weeks later Jack wrote again to Warnie:

I have said that the [evacuated] children are 'nice', and so they are. But modern children are poor creatures. They keep on coming to Maureen and asking 'What shall we do now?' She tells them to play tennis, or mend their stockings, or write home: and when that is done they come and ask again. Shades of our own childhood! …

One of the worst features of this war is the spectral feeling of all having happened before. As Dyson said, 'When you read the headlines (French advance – British steam ship sunk) you feel as if you'd had a delightful dream during the last war and woken up to find it still going on' … If one could only hibernate. More and more sleep seems to me the best thing – short of waking up and finding yourself safely dead and not quite damned.

Letters

Of all Lewis's series of radio talks, *Christian Behaviour* (which was to become Book III of *Mere Christianity*), if perhaps the easiest for lay people to understand, was perhaps also the most difficult to accept, since it dealt with putting into practice what Christianity was really teaching on subjects such as morality, marriage, forgiveness and charity.

According to Christian teachers, the essential vice, the utmost evil, is Pride. Unchastity, anger, greed, drunkenness, and all that, are mere fleabites in comparison: Pride leads to every other vice: it is the complete anti-God state of mind ... Each person's pride is in competition with everyone else's pride. It is because I wanted to be the big noise at the party that I am so annoyed at someone else being the big noise. Two of a trade never agree. Now what you want to get clear is that Pride is essentially competitive *– is competitive by its very nature – while the other vices are competitive only, so to speak, by accident. Pride gets no pleasure out of having something, only out of having more of it than the next man ...*

The Christians are right: it is Pride which has been the chief cause of misery in every nation and every family since the world began. Other vices may sometimes bring people together: you may find good fellowship and jokes and friendliness among drunken people or unchaste people. But pride always means enmity – it is *enmity. And not only enmity between man and man, but enmity to God ...*

As long as you are proud you cannot know God. A proud man is always looking down on things and people: and, of course, as long as you are looking down, you cannot see something that is above you ...

If anyone would like to acquire humility, I can, I think, tell him the first step. The first step is to realize that one is proud. And a biggish step, too. At least, nothing whatever can be done before it. If you think you are not conceited, it means you are very conceited indeed.

'Christian Behaviour' in Mere Christianity

Soon after war broke out in 1939, all fit young men and women – including, of course, those studying at Oxford – knew that before long they might be required to join one of the armed forces. Many of the undergraduates looked for guidance on the whole subject of war and learning and, three weeks after the outbreak of war, Lewis preached a sermon entitled 'Learning in Wartime' in the Church of St Mary the Virgin.

A university is a society for the pursuit of learning. As students, you will be expected to make yourselves, or to start making yourselves, into what the Middle Ages called clerks: into philosophers, scientists, scholars, critics or historians. And at first sight this seems to be an odd thing to do during a great war … Even if we ourselves should happen not to be interrupted by death or military service, why should we – indeed how can we – continue to take an interest in these placid occupations when the lives of our friends and the liberties of Europe are in the balance? …

The war creates no absolutely new situation: it simply aggravates the permanent human situation so that we can no longer ignore it. Human life has always been lived on the edge of a precipice. Human culture has always had to exist under the shadow of something infinitely more important than itself. If men had postponed the search for knowledge and beauty until they were secure, the search would never have begun …

Before I became a Christian I do not think I fully realized that one's life, after conversion, would inevitably consist in doing most of the same things one had been doing before: one hopes, in a new spirit, but still the same things … Neither conversion nor enlistment in the army is really going to obliterate our human life … The learned life … is, for some, a duty. At the moment it looks as if it were your duty. I am well aware that there may seem to be an almost comic discrepancy between the high issues we have been considering and the immediate task you may be set down to, such as Anglo-Saxon sound laws or chemical formulae. But there is a similar shock awaiting us in every vocation – a young priest finds himself involved in choir treats, and a young subaltern in accounting for pots of jam. It is well that it should be so. It weeds out the vain, windy people and keeps in those who are both humble and tough. But the peculiar difficulty imposed on you by the war is another matter: and of it I would again repeat, what I have been saying in one form or another ever since I started – do not let your nerves and emotions lead you into thinking your predicament more abnormal than it really is … War threatens us with death and pain. No man – and especially no Christian who remembers Gethsemane – need try to attain a stoic indifference about these things …

What does war do to death? It certainly does not make it more frequent: 100 per cent of us die and the percentage cannot be increased … Yet war does do something to death. It forces us to remember it … War makes death real to us: and that would have been regarded as one of its blessings by most of the great Christians of the past. They thought it good for us to be always aware of our mortality. I am inclined to think they were right. All the animal life in us, all schemes of happiness that centred in this world, were always doomed to a final frustration. In ordinary times only a wise man can realize it. Now the stupidest of us knows. We see unmistakably the sort of universe in which we have all along been living, and must come to terms with it. If we had foolish un-Christian hopes about human culture, they are now shattered. If we thought we were building up a heaven on earth, if we looked for something that would turn the present world from a place of pilgrimage into a permanent city satisfying the soul of man, we are disillusioned, and not a moment too soon. But if we thought that for some souls, and at some times, the life of learning, humbly offered to God, was, in its own small way, one of the appointed approaches to the divine reality and the divine beauty which we hope to enjoy hereafter, we can think so still.

'Learning in Wartime' in Fern-seed and Elephants

October

OCTOBER IS THE MONTH WHEN 'REAL' autumn sets in, when animals begin to prepare seriously for hibernation, and golden leaves fall from the trees. In Lewis's day (before central heating was widely in use in Britain) October was the time when people stocked up with logs and coal, and changed the flowery cotton curtains of summer for the thicker, draught-excluding ones of winter. October is the time, too, when the Michaelmas Term gets into its stride in the universities.

It is also traditionally the month when publishers produce their 'good books' in time for the Christmas market, and so was the month when several of Lewis's own works were published, including *The Problem of Pain* (1940), *Beyond Personality* (1944) and *The Lion, the Witch and the Wardrobe* (1950).

October also marked other important events in Lewis's life: the start of his lectures on 'The Romance of the Rose and Its Successors' in 1918; the move to The Kilns in 1930; the last Thursday evening meeting of The Inklings in 1949; and two stages of Joy's illness – when she went into hospital with cancer in 1956, and when, after a period of remission, the cancer returned in 1959.

When Jack Lewis joined the army in 1917 he met Paddy Moore, and the two friends later promised each other that if one was killed in action the survivor would take care of the dead one's parent. Paddy was killed in March 1918, and Jack cared for his mother until her death in January 1951. In October 1930 Jack, Mrs Moore and her daughter Maureen moved into The Kilns. Some 30 years later, he wrote in a letter:

I think I share to excess your feelings about a move. By nature I demand from the arrangements of this world just that permanence which God has expressly refused to give them. It is not merely the nuisance and expense of any big change in one's way of life that I dread, it is also the psychological uprooting and the feeling – to me or to you intensely unwelcome – of having ended a chapter. One more portion of myself slipping away into the past. I would like everything to be immemorial – to have the same old horizons, the same garden, the same smells and sounds, always there, changeless. The old wine is to me always better. That is, I desire the 'abiding city' where I well know it is not and ought not to be found. I suppose all these changes should prepare us for the greater change which has drawn nearer even since I began this letter. We must 'sit light' not only to life itself but to all its phases. The useless word is 'encore'.

In 1924 Lewis, aged 25, gave his first lecture in the University of Oxford, on 'The Good, its position among values'. He wrote to his father about his preparations for it:

I am plodding on with my fourteen lectures … I think I must take the plunge from the very beginning and learn to talk, *not to recite. I practise continually, expanding my notes to imaginary audiences, but of course it is difficult to be quite sure what will fill an hour … The laborious part is the continual verifying of references and* quoting *… And of course when one is trying to* teach *one can take nothing for granted …*

The day after he had given the lecture Lewis sent his father a note:

My maiden lecture yesterday went off all right in a sense – the only difficulty was the audience. They put me down for the same time at which a much more important lecture by an established man was being held elsewhere … Four people turned up … Otherwise everything goes well. All my new colleagues are kindness itself …

Letters

Lewis wrote seven books in *The Chronicles of Narnia*, of which *The Lion, the Witch and the Wardrobe* was the first. It is the story of four children evacuated during the Second World War and sent to stay with an old professor. In his house they discover a wardrobe which is the entrance to Narnia, where they join in the battle of good against evil, led by the good lion Aslan. The book was published in October 1950, and is still enchanting children today.

The Professor said, 'If there really is a door in this house that leads to some other world (and I should warn you that this is a very strange house, and even I know very little about it) – if, as I say, [Lucy] had got into another world, I should not be at all surprised to find that the other world had a separate time of its own; so that however long you stayed there it would never take up any of our time.'

'But do you really mean, sir,' said Peter, 'that there could be other worlds – all over the place, just round the corner – like that?'

'Nothing is more probable,' said the Professor …

The Beaver … added in a low whisper – 'They say Aslan is on the move – perhaps has already landed.' And now a very curious thing happened. None of the children knew who Aslan was any more than you do; but the moment the Beaver had spoken these words everyone felt quite different. Perhaps it has sometimes happened to you in a dream that someone says something which you don't understand but in the dream it feels as if it has some enormous meaning – either a terrifying one which turns the whole dream into a nightmare or else a lovely meaning too lovely to put into words, which makes the dream so beautiful that you remember it all your life and are always wishing you could get into that dream again. It was like that now. At the name of Aslan each one of the children felt something jump in its inside. Edmund felt a sensation of mysterious horror. Peter felt suddenly brave and adventurous. Susan felt as if some delicious smell or some delightful strain of music had just floated by her. And Lucy got the feeling you have when you wake up in the morning and realize that it is the beginning of the holidays or the beginning of Summer.

The Lion, the Witch and the Wardrobe

The first work on Christian beliefs that Lewis wrote was *The Problem of Pain* (published in October 1940), which looked at how a good and loving God could 'allow' good people to suffer. In France during the First World War, Lewis had felt that 'a just God that cares for earthly pain' was only a dream, and rebelled against such a God. Now, as a Christian, he tries to present the reality of divine goodness and to lead his readers to a sense of personal sin.

God whispers to us in our pleasures, speaks in our conscience, but shouts in our pain: it is His megaphone to rouse a deaf world. A bad man, happy, is a man without the least inkling that his actions do not 'answer', that they are not in accord with the laws of the universe.

A perception of this truth lies at the back of the universal human feeling that bad men ought to suffer. It is no use turning up our noses at this feeling, as if it were wholly base. On its mildest level it appeals to everyone's sense of justice …

When our ancestors referred to pains and sorrows as God's 'vengeance' upon sin they were not necessarily attributing evil passions to God; they may have been recognizing the good element in the idea of retribution. Until the evil man finds evil unmistakably present in his existence, in the form of pain, he is enclosed in illusion. Once pain has roused him, he knows that he is in some way 'up against' the real universe: he either rebels (with the possibility of a clearer issue and deeper repentance at some later stage) or else makes some real attempt at an adjustment, which, if pursued, will lead him to religion … No doubt Pain as God's megaphone is a terrible instrument; it may lead to final and unrepented rebellion. But it gives the only opportunity the bad man can have for amendment. It removes the veil; it plants the flag of truth within the fortress of a rebel soul …

What then can God do in our interests but make 'our own life' agreeable to us, and take away the plausible source of false happiness? It is just there, where God's providence seems at first to be most cruel, that the Divine humility, the stooping down of the Highest, most deserves praise. We are perplexed to see misfortune falling upon decent, inoffensive, worthy people … on those who have worked so hard, and so honestly, for their modest stock of happiness and now seem to be entering on the enjoyment of it with the fullest right. How can I say with sufficient tenderness what here needs to be said? … God, who made these deserving people, may really be right when He thinks that their modest prosperity and the happiness of their children are not enough to make them blessed: that all this must fall from them in the end, and that if they have not learned to know Him they will be wretched. And therefore He troubles them, warning them in advance of an insufficiency that one day they will have to discover … And this illusion of self-sufficiency may be at its strongest in some very honest, kindly, and temperate people, and on such people, therefore, misfortune must fall.

The Problem of Pain

In October 1956 pain of a terrible kind came to Jack's own door, when Joy Davidman was taken to the Wingfield-Morris Hospital suffering from cancer. In November Jack wrote to Arthur Greeves.

Joy is in hospital, suffering from cancer. The prospects are (1) A tiny 100th chance of ultimate cure. (2) A reasonable probability of some years more of (tolerable) life. (3) A real danger that she may die in a few months.

It will be a great tragedy for me to lose her. In the meantime, if she gets over this bout and emerges from hospital she will no longer be fit to live alone so she must come and live here. That means (in order to avoid scandal) that our marriage must shortly be published. W. has written to Janie and the Ewarts to tell them I am getting married, and I didn't want the news to take you by surprise. I know you will pray for her and for me: and for W., to whom also, the loss if we lose her, will be great.

Letters

Lewis's last series of radio talks, *Beyond Personality*, went out early in 1944 and was published as a book in September of that year, later becoming Book IV of *Mere Christianity*. For some reason the BBC scheduled the talks for 10.20 p.m., and as Lewis could not be away from Oxford on those nights, the talks were recorded on disks, one of which still exists.

Now the point in Christianity which gives us the greatest shock is the statement that by attaching ourselves to Christ, we can 'become Sons of God'. One asks 'Aren't we Sons of God already? Surely the fatherhood of God is one of the main Christian ideas?' Well, in a certain sense, no doubt we are sons of God already. I mean, God has brought us into existence and loves us and looks after us, and in that way is like a father. But when the Bible talks of our 'becoming' Sons of God, obviously it must mean something different. And that brings us up against the very centre of Theology.

One of the creeds says that Christ is the Son of God 'begotten, not created'; and it adds 'begotten by His Father before all worlds' … We are not now thinking about the Virgin Birth. We are thinking about something that happened before Nature was created at all, before time began. 'Before all worlds' Christ is begotten, not created. What does it mean?

We don't use the words begetting *or* begotten *much in modern English, but everyone still knows what they mean. To beget is to become the father of: to create is to make. And the difference is this. When you beget, you beget something of the same kind as yourself. A man begets human babies, a beaver begets little beavers, and a bird begets eggs which turn into little birds. But when you make, you make something of a different kind from yourself. A bird makes a nest, a beaver builds a dam, a man makes a wireless set – or he may make something more like himself than a wireless set: say, a statue. If he is a clever enough carver he may make a statue which is very like a man indeed. But, of course, it is not a real man; it only looks like one. It cannot breathe or think. It is not alive.*

Now that is the first thing to get clear. What God begets is God; just as what man begets is man. What God creates is not God; just as what man makes is not man. That is why men are not Sons of God in the sense that Christ is. They may be like God in certain ways, but they are not things of the same kind. They are more like statues or pictures of God …

A statue has the shape of a man but is not alive. In the same way, man has … the 'shape' or likeness of God, but he has not got the kind of life God has … When we come to man, the highest of the animals, we get the completest resemblance to God which we know of …

But what man, in his natural condition, has not got, is Spiritual life – the higher and different sort of life that exists in God. We use the same word life *for both: but if you thought that both must therefore be the same sort of thing, that would be like thinking that the 'greatness' of space and the 'greatness' of God were the same sort of greatness. In reality, the difference between Biological life and Spiritual life is so important that I am going to give them two distinct names. The Biological sort which comes to us through Nature, and which (like everything else in Nature) is always tending to run down and decay so that it can only be kept up by incessant subsidies from Nature in the form of air, water, food, etc., is* Bios. *The Spiritual life which is in God from all eternity, and which made the whole natural universe, is* Zoe. Bios *has, to be sure, a certain shadowy or symbolic resemblance to* Zoe: *but only the sort of resemblance there is between a photo and a place, or a statue and a man. A man who changed from having* Bios *to having* Zoe *would have gone through as big a change as a statue which changed from being a carved stone to being a real man.*

And that is precisely what Christianity is about. This world is a great sculptor's shop. We are the statues and there is a rumour going round the shop that some of us are some day going to come to life.

'Beyond Personality' in Mere Christianity

Although he was a brilliant academic with his mind 'on higher things', Jack Lewis was also an ordinary man with many of the same problems and worries as everyone else. Here, in a letter to an American friend who had recently visited him, Jack writes about the onset of old age and how it affects almost everything people do.

You are a bit further on the road than I am and will probably smile at a man whose fifty-first birthday is still several weeks ahead ... Yet why? The realization must begin *sometime. In one way, of course (no, in two) it began much earlier. (1) With the growing realization that there were a great many things one would never have time to do. Those golden days when one could still think it possible that one might some time take up a quite new study: say, Persian, or geology, were now definitely over. (2) Harder to express, I mean, the end of that period when every goal, besides being itself, was an earnest or promise of much more to come. Like a pretty girl at her first dance: valued not chiefly for itself but as the prelude to a whole new world. Do you remember the time when every pleasure (say, the smell of a hayfield or a country walk, or a swim) was big with futurity and bore on its face the notice 'Lots more where I came from'? Well, there's a change from that to the period when they all begin to say 'Make the most of me: my predecessors outnumber my successors.'*

Both these two feelings – the twitch of the tether and the loss of promise – I have had for a long time. What has come lately is much harsher – the arctic wind of the future catching one, so to speak, at a corner. The particular corner was the sharp realization that I shall be compulsorily 'retired' in 1959, and the infernal nuisance (to put it no higher) of patching up some new sort of life somewhere ...

Have you ever thought what it would be like if (all other things remaining as they are) old age and death had been made optional? All other things remaining: i.e. it would still be true that our real destiny was elsewhere, that we have no abiding city here and no true happiness, but *the unhitching from this life was left to be accomplished by our own will as an act of obedience and faith. I suppose the percentage of di-ers would be about the same as the percentage of Trappists now.*

I am therefore (with some help from the weather and rheumatism!) trying to profit by this new realization of my mortality. To begin to die, to loosen a few of the tentacles which the octopus-world has fastened on one. But of course it is continuings, not beginnings, that are the point. A good night's sleep, a sunny morning, a success with my next book – any of these will, I know alter the whole thing. One ought not to need the gloomy moments of life for beginning detachment, nor be re-entangled by the bright ones. One ought to be able to enjoy the bright ones to the full and at that very moment have the perfect readiness to leave them, confident that what calls one away is better...

Letters

On 20 October 1949 the last Thursday evening meeting of The Inklings was held. In a letter to his brother (an Inkling himself) Jack recalls one meeting of the group.

I had a pleasant evening on Thursday with Williams, Tolkien, and Wrenn, during which Wrenn almost seriously expressed a strong wish to burn Williams, or at least maintained that conversation with Williams enabled him to understand how inquisitors had felt it right to burn people ... The occasion was a discussion of the most distressing text in the Bible ('narrow is the way and few they be that find it') and whether one really could believe in a universe where the majority were damned and also in the goodness of God ... The general sense of the meeting was in favour of a view on the lines taken in Pastor Pastorium *– that Our Lord's replies are never straight answers and never gratify curiosity, and that whatever this one meant its purpose was certainly not statistical ...*

Letters

November

A COLD AND GENERALLY WET MONTH IN ENGLAND, November used to be infamous for its thick fogs, brought about not only by the dampness and the drop in temperature but also by the smoke from the numerous industrial chimneys and domestic coal fires by which the nation tried to maintain its commerce and its comfort. The fogs have virtually gone now, but the cold dampness remains, and November is not a comfortable month.

In Lewis's life, as usual good and bad were mixed: in 1917 he went as a young soldier to the muddy hell of the trenches of France, feeling that death would be the likely outcome; in 1944 the first instalment of *The Great Divorce* appeared; and in 1952 Jack dined twice with Joy in Oxford.

November was also the month which saw the birth of Lewis in 1898 and his death in 1963, a few days before his sixty-fifth birthday. The extract about his death is the only one in this book not written by him, but is by his brother Warnie.

On 29 November 1898 Clive Staples (Jack) Lewis was born in Belfast, in the family home at Dundela Villas.

I was born in the winter of 1898 at Belfast, the son of a solicitor and of a clergyman's daughter. My parents had only two children, both sons, and I was the younger by about three years … In addition to good parents, good food, and a garden (which then seemed large) to play in, I began life with two other blessings. One was our nurse, Lizzie Endicott, in whom even the exacting memory of childhood can discover no flaw – nothing but kindness, gaiety, and good sense … The other blessing was my brother. Though three years my senior, he never seemed to be an elder brother; we were allies, not to say confederates, from the first.

Surprised by Joy

On 17 November 1917 Jack Lewis was sent to France, arriving at the trenches on 29 November, his nineteenth birthday. His brother was a professional soldier and better prepared for the horrors of actual conflict, but Jack's fairly brief experience of military action was enough to instil in him a lifelong dislike of war and its futility. Later he wrote of this period:

I passed through the ordinary course of training (a mild affair in those days …) and was commissioned as a Second Lieutenant in the Somerset Light Infantry, the old XIIIth Foot. I arrived in the front line trenches on my nineteenth birthday, saw most of my service in the villages before Arras – Fampoux and Monchy – and was wounded at Mt Bernenchon, near Lillers, in April 1918.

I am surprised that I did not dislike the army more. It was, of course, detestable. But the words 'of course' drew the sting … One did not expect to like it. Nobody pretended to like it. Everyone you met took it for granted that the whole thing was an odious necessity, a ghastly interruption of rational life. And that made all the difference …

On my very first night in France, in a vast marquee or drill hall where about a hundred officers were to sleep on plank beds, two middle-aged Canadians at once took charge of me and treated me, not like a son (that might have given offence) but like a long-lost friend. Blessings upon them! … Every few days one seemed to meet a scholar, an original, a poet, a cheery buffoon, a raconteur, or at the least a man of good will.

Through the winter, weariness and water were our chief enemies. I have gone to sleep marching and woken again and found myself marching still. One walked in the trenches in thigh gum-boots with water above the knee; one remembers the icy stream welling up inside the boot when you punctured it on concealed barbed wire. Familiarity both with the very old and the very recent dead confirmed that view of corpses which had been formed the moment I saw my dead mother. I came to know and pity and reverence the ordinary man: particularly dear Sergeant Ayres, who was (I suppose) killed by the same shell that wounded me. I was a futile officer (they gave commissions too easily then), a puppet moved about by him, and he turned this ridiculous and painful relation into something beautiful, became to me almost like a father. But for the rest, the war – the frights, the cold, the smell of H.E. [High Explosives], the horribly smashed men still moving like half-crushed beetles, the sitting or standing corpses, the landscape of sheer earth without a blade of grass, the boots worn day and night till they seemed to grow to your feet – all this shows rarely and faintly in memory. It is too cut off from the rest of my experience and often seems to have happened to someone else. It is even in a way unimportant. One imaginative moment seems now to matter more than the realities that followed. It was the first bullet I heard – so far from me that it 'whined' like a journalist's or a peace-time poet's bullet. At that moment there was something not exactly like fear, much less like indifference: a little quavering signal that said, 'This is War. This is what Homer wrote about.'

Surprised by Joy

In November 1944 the first instalment of *The Great Divorce* appeared in a church magazine called *The Guardian*. It had been taking shape in Lewis's mind for several years – some of the ideas had already appeared in two poems, in *The Pilgrim's Regress* and in *The Problem of Pain* – and Jack read it to The Inklings. At one stage called *Who Goes Home?* (the cry used each night at the closing of the House of Commons), the book is Lewis's allegory on Heaven and Hell.

I seemed to be standing in a bus queue by the side of a long, mean street. Evening was just closing in and it was raining. I had been wandering for hours in similar mean streets, always in the rain and always in evening twilight. Time seemed to have paused on that dismal moment when only a few shops have lit up and it is not yet dark enough for their windows to look cheering. And just as the evening never advanced to night, so my walking had never brought me to the better parts of the town. However far I went I found only dingy lodging houses, small tobacconists, hoardings from which posters hung in rags, windowless warehouses, goods stations without trains, and bookshops of the sort that sell The Works of Aristotle. *I never met anyone. But for the little crowd at the bus stop, the whole town seemed to be empty. I think that was why I attached myself to the queue.*

I had a stroke of luck right away, for just as I took my stand a little waspish woman who would have been ahead of me snapped out at a man who seemed to be with her, 'Very well, then. I won't go at all. So there,' and left the queue … he also walked away. 'Come,' I thought, 'that's two places gained' … What with one thing and another the queue had reduced itself to manageable proportions long before the bus appeared.

It was a wonderful vehicle, blazing with golden light, heraldically coloured. The driver himself seemed full of light and he used only one hand to drive with. The other he waved before his face as if to fan away the greasy steam of the rain…

My fellow passengers fought like hens to get on board the bus though there was plenty of room for us all. I was the last to get in. The bus was only half full and I selected a seat at the back, well away from the others. But a tousle-headed youth at once came and sat down beside me …

'I thought you wouldn't mind my tacking on to you,' he said, 'for I've noticed that you feel just as I do about the present company. Why on earth they insist on coming, I can't imagine. They won't like it at all when we get there, and they'd really be much more comfortable at home. It's different for you and me.'

'Do they like *this place?' I asked.*

'As much as they'd like anything,' he answered. 'They've got cinemas and fish and chip shops and advertisements and all the sorts of things they want. The appalling lack of intellectual life doesn't worry them *... I've fooled about trying to wake people up here. I found a few fellows I'd known before and tried to form a little circle, but they all seem to have sunk to the level of their surroundings ... The last time I tried to read [them] some of my own stuff ... but wait a minute, I'd just like you to look at it.'*

Realizing with a shudder that what he was producing from his pocket was a thick wad of typewritten paper, I muttered something about not having my spectacles and exclaimed, 'Hullo! We've left the ground.'

It was true. Several hundred feet below us, already half hidden in the rain and mist, the wet roofs of the town appeared, spreading without a break as far as the eye could reach.

The Great Divorce

_____

_____

_____

_____

_____

_____

_____

Lewis admired and loved all his fellow Inklings, but Charles Williams had a special place in his affections. Williams worked for the Oxford University Press, first in London and then, when war came, in Oxford. He also wrote many novels and religious works, the best known of the latter being *The Descent of the Dove*. After one of Williams's lectures Jack wrote to Warnie.

On Tuesday evening I went to the JCR of St Hugh's to hear Williams read a paper – or rather not 'read' but 'spout' – i.e. to deliver without a single note a perfectly coherent and impassioned meditation, variegated with quotations in his incantatory manner. A most wonderful performance and impressed his audience, specially the young women, very much. And it really is remarkable how that ugly, almost simian, face, becomes transfigured.

Quoted in C.S. Lewis: A Companion and Guide

In the Preface to *Essays Presented to Charles Williams*, Jack wrote:

Our friendship rapidly grew inward to the bone. Until 1939 that friendship had to subsist on occasional meetings, though, even thus, he had already become as dear to all my Oxford friends as he was to me. There were many meetings both in my rooms at Magdalen and in Williams's tiny office at Amen House …

But in 1939 the Oxford University Press, and he with it, was evacuated to Oxford. From that time until his death we met one another about twice a week, sometimes more … The removal to Oxford also produced other changes. The English Faculty was depleted by war, and Williams was soon making an Oxford reputation both as a lecturer and a private tutor …

In appearance he was tall, slim, and straight as a boy, though grey-haired. His face we thought ugly: I am not sure that the word 'monkey' has not been murmured in this context. But the moment he spoke it became, as was also said, like the face of an angel … a masculine angel, a spirit burning with intelligence and charity … There was something of recklessness, something even of panache, *in his gait … He always carried his head in the air. When he lectured, wearing his gown, his presence was one of the stateliest I have ever seen.*

The Preface to Essays Presented to Charles Williams

On 22 November 1963, a few days before his sixty-fifth birthday, Clive Staples Lewis died. His beloved brother Warnie recalls that day:

Once again — as in the earliest days — we could turn for comfort only to each other. The wheel had come full circle: once again we were together in the little end room at home, shutting out from our talk the ever-present knowledge that the holidays were ending, that a new term fraught with unknown possibilities awaited us both.

Jack faced the prospect bravely and calmly. 'I have done all I wanted to do, and I'm ready to go,' he said to me one evening. Only once did he show any regret or reluctance: this was when I told him that the morning's mail included an invitation to deliver the Romanes lecture. An expression of sadness passed over his face, and there was a moment's silence: then, 'Send them a very polite refusal.'

Friday, 22nd November 1963, began much as other days: there was breakfast, then letters and the crossword puzzle. After lunch he fell asleep in his chair: I suggested that he would be more comfortable in bed, and he went there. At four I took in his tea and found him drowsy but comfortable. Our few words then were the last: at five-thirty I heard a crash and ran in, to find him lying unconscious at the foot of his bed. He ceased to breathe some three or four minutes later.

Memoir *by W.H. Lewis*

December

AS THE YEAR COMES TO A close, and the days are shortened by late mornings and early evenings, the cold ensures that any outdoor activity is done speedily. Taking a bracing walk in the crisp air, enjoying the bare outlines of trees set starkly against a pale blue sky or a sometimes surprisingly fiery sunset, is a treat which many people relish, and Jack Lewis was one of them. Getting back to his study after such a walk, refreshed in both mind and body, he was ready for tea and then an evening of reading or talking with friends.

December 1916 was the month in which Jack first visited Oxford, a place which was to be so important to him in later life, and it was in December 1954 that Jack gave his last tutorial at Magdalen College. At the very end of 1926 Jack and Warnie spent their last time together with their father in 'Little Lea', before Warnie sailed to serve in the army in China. In December 1952 Joy Davidman spent two weeks at The Kilns with Jack and Warnie, followed a year later by a shorter visit with her two sons.

Although written earlier in the year, it seems fitting to end this collection with three brief farewell notes Jack wrote shortly before his death.

Jack's boyhood Christian beliefs had been eroded by his time at school in England, but in order not to shock and dismay his father, who expected him to do what all good Christian boys did, in December 1914 Jack, aged 16, allowed himself to be confirmed in the Church of Ireland. This was an act of cowardice that he was to regret for many years.

My relations to my father help to explain (I am not suggesting that they excuse) one of the worst acts of my life. I allowed myself to be prepared for confirmation, and confirmed, and to make my first Communion, in total disbelief, acting a part, eating and drinking my own condemnation. As Johnson points out, where courage is not, no other virtue can survive except by accident. Cowardice drove me into hypocrisy and hypocrisy into blasphemy. It is true that I did not and could not then know the real nature of the thing I was doing: but I knew very well that I was acting a lie with the greatest possible solemnity. It seemed to me impossible to tell my father my real views. Not that he would have stormed and thundered like the traditional orthodox parent … But it would have been quite impossible to drive into his head my real position. The thread would have been lost almost at once, and the answer implicit in all the quotations, anecdotes, and reminiscences which would have poured over me would have been one I then valued not a straw – the beauty of the Authorized Version, the beauty of the Christian tradition and sentiment and character. And later, when this failed, when I still tried to make my exact points clear, there would have been anger between us, thunder from him and a thin peevish rattle from me. Nor could the subject, once raised, ever have been dropped again. All this, of course, ought to have been dared rather than the thing I did. But at the time it seemed to me impossible.

Surprised by Joy

Lewis's hope of finding 'Joy' continued during his time at Bookham with Mr Kirkpatrick, and he kept trying hard to recapture the feeling, but always in vain – it had to come naturally and it had to take him unawares. One December day in 1915 it did indeed come again.

At that very moment there arose the memory of a place and time at which I had tasted Joy with unusual fullness. It had been a particular hill walk on a morning of white mist. The other volumes of The Ring … *had just arrived as a Christmas present from my father, and the thought of all the reading before me, mixed with the coldness and loneliness of the hillside, the drops of moisture on every branch, and the distant murmur of the concealed town, had produced a longing (yet it was also fruition) which had flowed over from the mind and seemed to involve the whole body. That walk I now remembered. It seemed to me that I had tasted heaven then. If only such a moment could return! But what I never realized was that it had returned – that the remembering of that walk was itself a new experience of just the same kind.*

Surprised by Joy

In December 1916, after two years of study with W.T. Kirkpatrick, Jack Lewis went to Oxford in order to sit the scholarship exam which would secure his entrance to the university. He knew by now that he wanted to be a don, though he also realized that the War could effectively put paid to such plans, either temporarily or permanently. It was his first visit to the city.

It was late in the winter term of 1916 that I went to Oxford to sit for my scholarship examination. Boys who have faced this ordeal in peace time will not easily imagine the indifference with which I went. This does not mean that I underestimated the importance (in one sense) of succeeding. I knew very well by now that there was hardly any position in the world save that of a don in which I was fitted to earn a living, and that I was staking everything on a game in which few won and hundreds lost. As Kirk had said of me in a letter to my father (I did not, of course, see it till many years later), 'You may make a writer or a scholar of him, but you'll not make anything else' … And I knew this myself; sometimes it terrified me. What blunted the edge of it now was that whether I won a scholarship or no I should next year go into the army; and even a temper more sanguine than mine could feel in 1916 that an infantry subaltern would be insane to waste anxiety on anything so hypothetical as his post-war life …

My first taste of Oxford was comical enough. I had made no arrangements about quarters and, having no more luggage than I could carry in my hand, I sallied out of the railway station on foot to find either a lodging house or a cheap hotel; all agog for 'dreaming spires' and 'last enchantments' … Towns always show their worst face to the railway … Only when it became very obvious that there was very little town left ahead of me, that I was in fact getting to open country, did I turn round and look. There, behind me, far away, never more beautiful since, was the fabled cluster of spires and towers. I had come out of the station on the wrong side and been all this time walking into what was even then the mean and sprawling suburb of Botley. I did not see to what extent this little adventure was an allegory of my whole life …

It was very cold and next day snow began to fall, turning pinnacles into wedding-cake decorations. The examination was held in the Hall of Oriel, and we all wrote in greatcoats and mufflers and wearing at least our left-hand gloves. The

Provost, old Phelps, gave out the papers. I remember very little about them, but I suppose I was outshone in pure classics by many of my rivals and succeeded on my general knowledge and dialectics. I had the impression that I was doing badly … It was a blessed state to be in, but for the moment depressing … When I arrived home I told my father that I had almost certainly failed. It was an admission calculated to bring out all his tenderness and chivalry. The man who could not understand a boy's taking his own possible, or probable, death into account could very well understand a child's disappointment. Not a word was now heard of expenses and difficulties; nothing but consolation, reassurance and affection. Then, almost on Christmas Eve, we heard that 'Univ.' [University College] had elected me.

In the Trinity (Summer) Term of 1917, Lewis went into residence in Oxford.

I was less than a term at Univ. when my papers came through and I enlisted; and the conditions made it a most abnormal term. Half the College had been converted into a hospital and was in the hands of the RAMC. In the remaining portion lived a tiny community of undergraduates … Small though our numbers were (about eight) we were rather distinguished, for we included E.V. Gordon, afterwards Professor of English at Manchester, and A.C. Ewing, the Cambridge philosopher; also that witty and kindly man, Theobald Butler, skilled in turning the most lurid limericks into Greek verse. I enjoyed myself greatly; but it bore little resemblance to normal undergraduate life and was for me an unsettled, excited, and generally useless period. Then came the army. By a remarkable turn of fate this did not mean removal from Oxford. I was drafted into a Cadet Battalion whose billet was Keble.

Surprised by Joy

Jack Lewis was often asked what he meant by the word 'allegory', and his answer was that it needed defining in each context in which it was used. Many people said that his science-fiction novels and *The Chronicles of Narnia* were allegories, but he always denied that. Allegory was one of Lewis's favourite things, and in 1958 he wrote to a correspondent who had asked him about it.

By an allegory I mean a composition (whether pictorial or literary) in which immaterial realities are represented by feigned physical objects e.g. a pictured Cupid allegorically represents erotic love (which in reality is an experience, not an object occupying a given area of space) or, in Bunyan a giant represents Despair.

If Aslan represented the immaterial Deity in the same way in which Giant Despair represents Despair, he would be an allegorical figure. In reality however he is an invention giving an imaginary answer to the question 'What might Christ become like if there really were a world like Narnia and He chose to be incarnate and die and rise again in that world as He actually has done in ours?' This is not allegory at all. So in Perelandra. *This also works out a* supposition. *('Suppose, even now, in some other planet there were a first couple undergoing the same that Adam and Eve underwent here, but successfully.')*

Allegory and such supposals differ because they mix the real and the unreal in different ways. Bunyan's picture of Giant Despair does not start from supposal at all. It is not a supposition but a fact *that despair can capture and imprison a human soul. What is unreal (fictional) is the giant, the castle, and the dungeon. The Incarnation of Christ in another world is mere supposal: but* granted *the supposition, He would really have been a physical object in that world as He was in Palestine, and His death on the Stone Table would have been a physical event no less than his death on Calvary. Similarly, if the angels (who I believe to be real beings in the actual universe) have that relation to the Pagan gods which they are assumed to have in* Perelandra, *they might* really *manifest themselves in real form as they did to Ransom. Again, Ransom (to some extent) plays the role of Christ not because he allegorically represents Him (as Cupid represents falling in love) but because in reality every real Christian is really called upon in some measure to* enact *Christ. Of course Ransom does this rather more spectacularly than most. But that does not mean that he does it allegorically. It only means that fiction (at any rate my kind of fiction) chooses extreme cases.*

There is no conscious connection between any of the phonetic elements in my 'Old Solar' words and those of any actual language. I am always playing with syllables and fitting them together (purely by ear) to see if I can hatch up new words that please me. I want them to have an emotional, not intellectual, suggestiveness: the heaviness of glund *for as huge a planet as Jupiter, the vibrating, tintillating quality of* vitritrilbia *for the subtlety of Mercury, the liquidity … of Maleldil. The only exception I am aware of is* hnau *which may (but I don't know) have been influenced by Greek* nous.

Letters

Jack Lewis kept up a vast correspondence with all kinds of people who had heard his broadcasts or read his books, and after the publication of *The Chronicles of Narnia*, these included a lot of children. In 1959 he wrote to an American schoolgirl who wanted some advice on writing.

1. *Turn off the radio.*
2. *Read all the good books you can, and avoid nearly all magazines.*
3. *Always write (and read) with the ear, not the eye. You should hear every sentence you write as if it was being read aloud or spoken. If it does not sound nice, try again.*
4. *Write about what really interests you, whether it is real things or imaginary things, and nothing else. (Notice this means that if you are interested* only *in writing you will never be a writer, because you will have nothing to write about …)*
5. *Take great pains to be* clear. *Remember that though you start by knowing what you mean, the reader doesn't, and a single ill-chosen word may lead him to a total misunderstanding. In a story it is terribly easy just to forget that you have not told the reader something that he needs to know – the whole picture is so clear in your own mind that you forget that it isn't the same in his.*
6. *When you give up a bit of work don't (unless it is hopelessly bad) throw it away. Put it in a drawer. It may come in useful later. Much of my best work, or what I think my best, is the re-writing of things begun and abandoned years earlier.*
7. *Don't use a typewriter. The noise will destroy your sense of rhythm, which still needs years of training.*
8. *Be sure you know the meaning (or meanings) of every word you use.*

Letters

Before he died in September 1963, Lewis wrote three notes, and they have been placed here, at the end of the December section, as his farewell to all his readers. The first was to his friend Sister Penelope, whom he had known since she first wrote to thank him for writing *Out of the Silent Planet* (one of his science-fiction books).

What a pleasant change to get a letter which does not *say the conventional things! I was unexpectedly revived from a long coma – and perhaps the almost continuous prayers of my friends did it – but it would have been a luxuriously easy passage and one almost (but* nella sua voluntade e nostra pace *– 'In His will is our peace') regrets having the door shut in one's face. Ought we to honour Lazarus rather than Stephen as the protomartyr? To be brought back and have all one's dying to do again* was rather hard.

If you die first, and if 'prison visiting' is allowed, come down and look me up in Purgatory. It is all rather fun – solemn fun – isn't it?

Letters

The second note was to the Master and Fellows of Magdalene College, Cambridge, where Lewis had spent his last few working years.

The ghosts of the wicked old women in Pope 'haunt the places where their honour died'. I am more fortunate, for I shall haunt the place whence the most valued of my honours came.

I am constantly with you in imagination. If in some twilit hour anyone sees a bald and bulky spectre in the Combination Room or the garden, don't get Simon to exorcise it, for it is a harmless wraith and means nothing but good.

If I loved you all less I should think much of being thus placed ('so were I equall'd with them in renown') beside Kipling and Eliot. But the closer and more domestic bond with Magdalene makes that side of it seem unimportant.

Letters

The third note was to another friend, Miss Jane Douglass.

Thanks for your kind note. Yes, Autumn is really the best of the seasons: and I'm not sure that old age isn't the best part of life. But of course, like Autumn, it doesn't last.

Letters

Notes

Notes

Acknowledgements

The Editor and Publishers are grateful for permission to use the following material, which is reproduced by permission of the copyright holders:

The Abolition of Man, C.S. Lewis: a Companion and Guide, Fern-seed and Elephants, The Four Loves, The Great Divorce, Letters to Malcolm: Chiefly on Prayer, The Lion, the Witch and the Wardrobe, Mere Christianity, Miracles, Narrative Poems, The Pilgrim's Regress, Poems, The Problem of Pain, Screwtape Proposes a Toast, The Screwtape Letters, Surprised by Joy and *Till We Have Faces* are reproduced with kind permission of HarperCollins*Publishers*.

The Letters of C.S. Lewis by kind permission of the Estates of C.S. Lewis and W.H. Lewis.
Letters to Children by kind permission of HarperCollins*Publishers*, and for Canada by Macmillan.
A Grief Observed by kind permission of Faber and Faber.

All items are the copyright of C.S. Lewis Pte Ltd.

Full details of the writings of C.S. Lewis can be found in *C.S. Lewis: A Companion and Guide* by Walter Hooper, published by HarperCollins*Publishers* in 1996.